Excel

Get the Results You Want!

HSC ESSAY WRITING MADE EASY

Stephen McLaren

PASCAL PRESS

Reprinted 1996, 1997, 1998, 2000
Second edition 2001
Reprinted 2002, 2003, 2004 (with minor revisions), 2006
Revised edition 2010
Reprinted 2011, 2012, 2013
Revised edition 2015
Reprinted 2016
Revised edition 2020
Reprinted 2022, 2024

ISBN 978 1 74125 688 8

Pascal Press
PO Box 250
Glebe NSW 2037
(02) 9198 1748

Publisher: Vivienne Joannou
Project editor: Mark Dixon
Edited by Ken Tate, Leanne Poll and Ian Rohr
Cover and typesetting by Origin Studio
Cartoons by Grant McAloon
Printed by Vivar Printing/Green Giant Press

Thanks to Sylvia Huntington for her helpful suggestions and patient reading.

Contents

Chapter-by-chapter contents

Preface to second edition

It is a great pleasure to introduce the second edition of this book, which has been comprehensively revised for the new HSC syllabus. As with the first edition, the focus stays on the HSC English syllabus, which remains a core compulsory subject. Writing skills are essential to each level of our academic development and I believe that this book is of equal value to English Extension students as it is to those who are studying other courses in English.

Given the continuing demand for the first edition since 1995, clearly there was a real need for help with the skills of formal writing. Under the new HSC this need remains. While the standards-referenced approach to assessment does not emphasise essay-writing skills as such, writing well pays off in every subject that involves formal writing or extended responses. That is because any extended response can only be as good as the quality of thought that informs it, and writing well, in its turn, helps you develop your understanding of the subject. Good, clear writing is the sign of a solid understanding of the topic.

Under the new HSC syllabus, students doing Standard English need to perform very well to achieve the top levels of assessment banding, whereas Advanced and Extension English students will find significant expectations of their composing skills. According to a key policy document:

> Students undertaking standard courses will have the opportunity to perform well up the scale, but they will be less likely to do so than those successfully undertaking more advanced work. Students undertaking more demanding studies, therefore, will be rewarded for their hard work and performance. The rewards, however, will not be automatic: they will depend on success in meeting the standards.
>
> (*Securing Their Future*, NSW Government, 1997, p. 24.)

Clearly the new HSC has been devised to reward achievement, and good writing is intrinsic to that endeavour in most subjects.

The revision has been very substantial. Two of the three sample essays are new, to reflect the new syllabus. They were composed for the Area of Study common to Standard and Advanced English, so will be of interest to most students. Sample questions, exercises and other references have all been updated to reflect the new syllabuses. I have retained the light tone of the original edition, and the use of contractions (*it's* rather than *it is*, *don't* rather than *do not*) but students will appreciate that academic writing follows different rules and that many teachers frown on the use of contractions.

Development of the new HSC involved much effort to identify key competencies and outcomes that are central to workplace readiness. I remain convinced that effective writing is one of the most important of these, and that taking time to develop one's writing skills remains one of the best investments for the future that any student can make.

Stephen McLaren

Note for 2004 reprint:

The sample essays, and most of the other examples in this book were couched according to the Common Area of Study for Standard and Advanced English for the 2001 English syllabus. While the Common Area of Study and the reading list do change periodically, the same principles exemplified here continue to apply. However, I have added some explanation as to how to apply similar techniques and approaches to different Areas of Study and prescribed texts. In addition, some examples have been changed, in addition to the updating of some topical references.

March 2004

Note for 2010 revision:

The announcement of a new set of prescribed texts for HSC English for the years 2009–12, together with significant changes in relation to the Common Area of Study, has prompted a major revision of the book. With the withdrawal of the prescribed stimulus booklet, greater emphasis may fall on student selection of texts relevant to the prescribed text. For this reason, a replacement sample essay has been supplied in Chapter 6, in which a variety of supplementary texts are addressed. Exam questions have often been reasonably broad in the past: the new sample essay illustrates an approach to meeting the requirements of a more 'closed' essay question where several topic keywords are specified. Previously, the concept to be explored in the Common Area of Study was narrowed into prescribed focuses, but these will not be used in 2009–12. Therefore I have supplied a new sample thesis essay also, in Chapter 7, in which syllabus themes are explored in some detail. The most dramatic change, however, is that for the first time a sample exam-style essay has also been furnished: this can be found in Chapter 9. Various other minor changes have been made throughout the book, and some examples have been updated to reflect the present list of HSC English electives and texts. In addition, I have incorporated some examples of a simple referencing method in two essays, in recognition of a growing interest in this question.

February 2010

Note for 2015 revision:

In this revision, the sample essay in Chapter 6 and the thesis essay have been replaced to reflect the prescribed texts for the years 2015–20. Most of the comments in the note for the 2010 revision also apply to the 2015 revision, except that only one topic keyword is found in the new Chapter 6 sample essay question. It is nonetheless a reasonably 'closed' question. Prescribed focuses continue not to be applied in the Common Area of Study.

February 2015

Note for 2020 revision:

The introduction of sweeping changes to the assessment of all courses from 2018 is accompanied by the introduction of new syllabuses in English, Mathematics, Science and History. Some interesting themes in these changes are the pursuit of depth in studies, a concerted effort to consider the varied needs of the very diverse population undertaking HSC studies each year, and addressing some Australian cross-curriculum priorities: Aboriginal and Torres Strait Islander histories and cultures, Australia's engagement with Asia, and Sustainability. As usual, the sample essay in Chapter 6 and the thesis essay have been updated. Special thanks to my publisher Vivienne Joannou for her dedication to keeping this book updated and available to a new generation of students.

January 2020

To the reader

This book offers:

- a practical, commonsense introduction to essay writing for beginners, starting from the ground up.
- an understanding of what writing essays is all about: not just what to do, but why!
- helpful exercises to build up your skills.
- sample essays, dissected, with explanations.
- many examples!
- an opportunity to develop essay-writing skills at the same time as you study.
- a detailed, step-by-step beginner's essay-writing method.
- special help with writing essays for English.

This book is designed for beginners, for people whose skills have become rusty, and for anyone struggling with essay writing. The methods described here have been used successfully not only with battling students, but also with middling and even top students wanting to realise more of their potential.

I have been teaching English and writing skills for many years now and this book is based on the lessons I have learnt from students themselves: about what problems they encounter and what they need to know. No magic solutions or shortcuts are offered here, but you will find plenty of help in these pages. In particular I seek to dispel some common myths:

- You have to be a 'born' writer.
- You can't *learn* to write.
- I'm a bad writer: I can't spell.

This book allows you to begin from your own level of skill, and to build up slowly.

HSC students

For many HSC students, essay writing is both the greatest stumbling block, and a key to success—not just now, but later in life too. This book demonstrates that you should begin your study effort as early as possible, and that you can combine essay-writing practice with study in different subjects, to 'kill two birds with one stone'. Particular attention is given to essays for HSC English because it is a compulsory subject.

What's in this book?

- Section one gives some essential background about study, the writing process, and essays in particular.
- Section two shows how to slowly build up your essay-writing skills, giving you practice with a number of microskills first, before bringing all those skills together in an organised approach.
- Section three describes ways of treating the specific requirements of essay writing for English.
- Section four looks at exam essays and gives some hints about the special requirements of other subjects.

How to use this book

- Write a little each day.
- Get a reader/mentor.
- Become your own mentor.
- Do your writing exercises on topics you are studying.

Development of essay-writing skills takes time and regular practice. It is better to write a little each day (for even as little as fifteen minutes) than to write for several hours once a week. Fix a set time for writing each day and stick to this, no matter what tempting diversions offer themselves. Turn your phone off, shut down social media alerts and all the other distractions that may bombard you, and lock yourself inside a room with a 'do not disturb sign' if you need to.

Writing is often a lonely business and can be especially hard for an underconfident person. One trap for beginners is to become too harsh a critic of your own writing, throwing out promising drafts and discarding good ideas, instead of refining and polishing those rough beginnings.

Another common trap is trying to rewrite an essay according to what you imagine the teacher wanted, what a friend has done, or based on some other piece you've just read (perhaps an essay sent to you by a friend or by a participant in an online forum).

Not everyone can afford a tutor but a good tutor can be invaluable. It will certainly be a great help to find a patient, supportive reader for your essay drafts: a parent, willing teacher or friend. You'll be surprised how much a perceptive reader can help you work through those ideas still trapped in a web of vague thoughts and hard-to-find words.

Or they can show you that what seems perfectly clear to you is not clear at all to the reader. Over time you will learn to criticise your own writings positively, and edit them more objectively, to become your own 'mentor', not tormentor.

Essays aren't just about words and writing; they're about your knowledge and thoughts. Writing also develops your understanding of topics; indeed, it is a skill that develops your mind! You don't have to wait to get a class essay before using this book—start doing the 'microskill' exercises in Chapter 4 now, then practise writing essays on topics you are currently studying, so that your understanding of study areas will grow as your skills do.

You can use this book for future reference too: if you are getting feedback from your teachers that your conclusions are weak or that you need to write topic sentences, you can refer back to these specific points and find help.

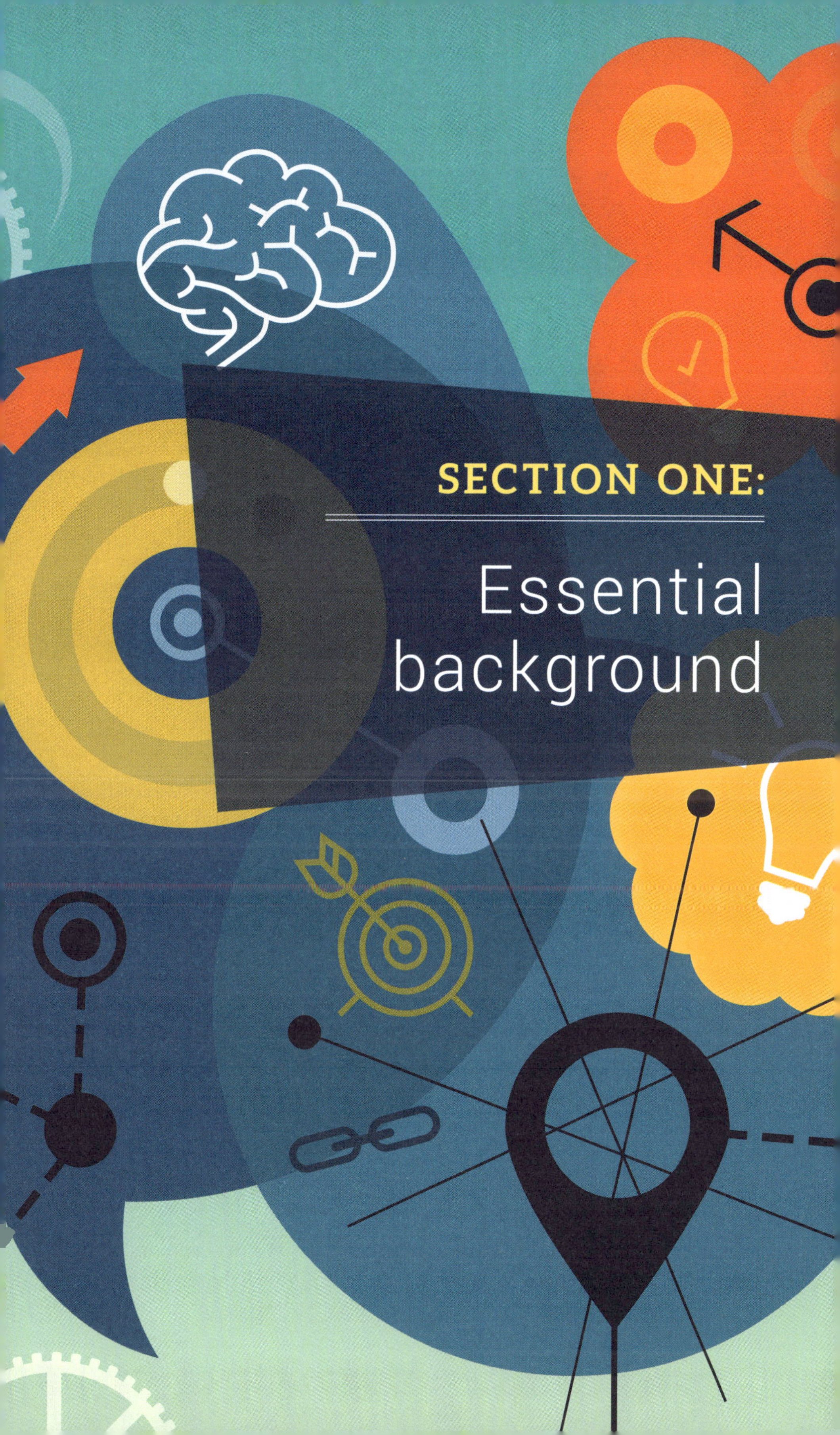
SECTION ONE:
Essential background

Staffroom gossip: common teacher complaints about students

Let's hear some choice gossip from the staffroom. About you!

Crime 1:

You don't answer the question (you use a prefabricated, one-size-fits-all essay, and pretend that this answers the question, or you just waffle on about anything vaguely related to the topic).

Crime 2:

You have a good understanding of the subject, but still 'can't write an essay' (structure's all over the place).

Crime 3:

You write too little (what you write is good, but how can I give you top marks if you don't say half as much as another student?).

Crime 4:

You keep repeating yourself instead of developing your ideas further (you've got nothing more to say, you're wasting paper and ink … and my time!).

Crime 5:

You have poor expression and use language badly (I can't even understand this!).

Crime 6:

You 'all write the same answer' (a bit of originality or imagination wouldn't go astray, in English at least).

Crime 7:

You can't spell.

You have probably committed some or all of these 'crimes'. The following chapters will help give you some insights into why these complaints are problems, and what to do about them. Please note that I have put spelling at the end of the heap … It is significant, but it's not the most important thing by any means. Some students think that if they can't spell, they can't write. Don't believe it; spelling is largely memory work, and definitely not a measure of your intelligence! But certainly, accurate spelling makes a good impression.

Experience has taught me that beginner essay writers most often need help in four main areas:

- how to study
- the process of writing
- requirements of an essay
- using language.

How to study

The quality of your essays depends on the quality of your study effort: you can't write in a vacuum. Although this is not a 'how to study' book, we look at broad study issues in Chapter 1, while Chapter 5 focuses on studying for essays. The thesis essay study technique for English is an advanced study method based on essays, and can also be adapted to other subjects (see Chapter 7).

The process of writing

Writing is a gradual process: we develop that polished draft over time, building those patchy starts into a structured argument. A rough first draft is not a failure but a beginning. The writing process is discussed in Chapter 2.

Requirements of an essay

Essays make many demands, and a general description of these begins in Chapter 3.

Using language

Language use is extremely important to writing. It improves with practice, draft by draft. Language is a subject vast enough to fill whole books. The focus here is restricted to a general awareness of language 'issues' such as clarity, word choice, and so on, rather than details of grammar and punctuation. Some of the more basic problems encountered by students are treated in this book but if you want to study language in detail, you should consult some of the many good reference books available on grammar, punctuation, and spelling.

It is easy to get carried away with the importance of grammatical, fluent English, but this book emphasises meaning first: it's possible to write a grammatically perfect sentence that doesn't mean anything, and you can't find exactly the right words to express your thoughts until you know what you are really trying to say! The famous theorist Noam Chomsky produced this sentence for us to contemplate: 'Colourless green dreams sleep furiously'. Grammatically speaking, the sentence is perfect, but not only does it not seem to mean anything, it even contradicts itself—how can green dreams be colourless?

Essay writing for English ...

This book devotes an entire section to English essays in particular. This is for several reasons:

- Many students find English the hardest subject; they complain that they don't understand what's expected of them.
- English is all about language. Essay writing helps develop your awareness of writing at the same time as you explore and develop ideas.

- A good essay in English uses all the fundamental skills that you could require in any subject, and once students get the hang of it, they usually notice an immediate improvement in essays for other subjects.
- The thesis essay approach discussed in Section three is a unique approach to English study that develops essay-writing skills, increases your understanding of English texts and topics, and helps prepare you for the exams.

... And beyond

As they used to say in the old Demtel ads: 'But there's more!'—the skills of writing you start to develop now will stand you in good stead when you go on to study at university or TAFE, and when you have to write letters and reports in your job. ('Communication skills' such as writing are much in demand with employers these days, a fact recognised in the new HSC syllabus.)

More importantly for the moment, increased proficiency in writing will help you enjoy your study better as your skills and your confidence increase.

1 Essays and study

Essay writing can be compared to mountain climbing:

- It's an act of exploration.
- It takes preparation.
- Planning is important.
- It takes practice and discipline.
- You need to be 'fit'.
- You need agility.
- Particular skills are needed.

Like mountain climbing, essay writing has its ups and downs. Luckily it's perfectly safe, so when you do suffer a mishap you can just try again. An organised climb is planned carefully, enjoys steady progress and works past all the obstacles and difficulties one by one. And don't be like those thrill seekers who try to race up the slopes in one day, the day before the deadline, and can't work out why they run out of puff, strain something, overlook something vitally important, get holed up in a dead end without time to find a better path, or simply seize up with stress.

The climb is hard work—I'm sorry, like a mountain, there's no way around it—but an organised approach will make it bearable and more rewarding.

Without this, your efforts will always be a bit of a scramble (in two senses of the word!) and you'll find it hard to get a secure foothold. With the necessary skills you can climb a very long way indeed, and the views from the top are just great! Honestly.

Exploration

Essay writing can and should be a learning process, a discovery of new territory. By writing about a subject, you will extend the frontiers of your understanding. You might find to your surprise that you've ended up writing a different essay to what you intended. Your ideas may have changed a lot, or even reversed completely in some cases, as you consider the evidence more carefully.

Preparation

You can't climb a mountain on an empty stomach; likewise, your mind requires good quality 'brain food': organised notes about your essay topics. Without sufficient knowledge, you can only write an empty essay.

Before planning your assault on 'Mount Everest', you need to research the job: just how tall, how treacherous, how cold is it up there? What gear will you need, what skills, how many provisions, how many team members? Be prepared!

Planning

It is preferable to plan any essay in advance, and this is essential in the exam room. However, it is possible to do some preliminary exploring before coming up with a plan.

Equipment

You need a good, quiet study environment: a comfortable chair and desk, with adequate lighting. Get a good dictionary, a thesaurus, lots of manila folders or other folders for all your notes. Of course, computers are superb writing machines, since they make it easy to write and rewrite. An internet connection also opens up the rich resources of the world wide web. However, be aware that the quality and reliability of websites varies greatly; also be very careful not to plagiarise, something that is far too easy to do when copy and paste is so readily available. 'Plagiarise' means to copy someone else's work without acknowledging the author. Even work that you download from the internet should be referenced in terms of the author, site name and URL, i.e. web address.

Practice and discipline

Consider yourself a kind of study 'athlete': set your goals, train hard to achieve them, and check regularly that you are making satisfactory progress. It is much better to study efficiently, with concentration, for short bursts of time, than to spend many hours staring out the window. I know, I've tried both ways myself!

Professional writers speak of developing 'writing muscles' in the brain by regular practice. Certainly, the more frequently you write, the stronger will be your skills. Use your time carefully: by studying efficiently, you can earn time enough for fun, rest and recreation. Start early, concentrate hard for short bursts of time, take frequent breaks, and reward yourself for achieving goals.

Fitness

Various factors combine to make you 'fit'. The main thing is to keep up the writing effort consistently. It's amazing how quickly our skills start to get rusty when we don't use them for a while. Regular writing will help keep those 'muscles' toned, so you can attack the final exams in peak condition.

Agility

Faced with a demanding or hard-to-understand question, there may be times when you'll find it handy to perform some mental gymnastics. Essay questions ask you to write about a topic from a *prescribed perspective:* that is, from a particular viewpoint, which you may or may not be familiar with, or feel comfortable with. Again, experience and practice will help you out with this. In general it is good to be flexible, ready to respond to whatever challenge you meet.

Particular skills

Essay writing brings together many separate skills, which we begin to build up in Chapter 4.

Pitfalls and false turns

Like climbing, writing can involve frustrating setbacks along the way: unexpected dead-ends, obstacles, twists in the path, cliffs that are too sheer. That's one reason to prepare in advance, rather than relying on the 'last night special', when it's too late to discover that you need additional information, or extra time to think, and so on.

Your studies in English and other subjects provide you with an opportunity to explore the world: to become aware of important issues in the modern world, to learn about great events in history, the lives of people in other places and other times, and the future that is emerging. The quality of your exploration and the enjoyment that you get out of it depend on you, your approach and your attitudes. You might as well make the most of it!

2 About writing

- *You can write!*
- You can *learn* to write!
- Writing means rewriting.
- The stages of writing:
  - 'Garble'
  - 'Clarify'
  - 'Edit'

You *can* write!

Students often tell me: 'I know what I'm trying to say but I just can't write it' or 'I just can't get my thoughts out onto paper'. Once they realise that words don't have to come out perfectly in the first draft, they usually start to make progress. Bad early experiences at home or school can cause poor self-esteem in very capable students.

No-one is a 'born' essay writer. The skill is like any other—acquired through practice and guidance. Those who take to it more quickly have usually done a lot of reading and writing already.

Your ability to express ideas and to develop them will grow as you master the essay form.

Anyone who can speak English uses language. And anyone who can use language can write.

Many English students complain that they find it impossible to find the 'right' answer. However, what you are required to do is develop your own. This takes confidence, and the systematic approach described in Chapter 7 will help you gain this.

You can *learn* to write!

It is not, as some people say, 'impossible to learn essay writing'. On the other hand, it's not as easy as some people say either. I've seen impatient people exclaiming: 'Look. You just write an introduction, follow it up with the body and finish with a conclusion, right? That's all there is to it'.

That sounds easy enough. It's just as easy to build a house too—just lay foundations, put up a frame, lay a roof on it, then fill up the walls and windows. Simple—we can all build houses now, can't we?

Obviously there are many other skills involved: the full job involves bricklaying, plumbing, sawing, designing and insulating ... Actually, essay writing starts to look pretty easy compared to housebuilding, but there are still a few 'tricks of the trade' you should try to master first! That's why we 'build up' to essay writing in this book by looking at basic skills first.

Writing means rewriting

- The essay is like a par 3–4 golf hole: it will usually take three to four 'strokes'—that is, drafts, to reach the goal. Even very experienced professional writers produce several drafts before the finished product is achieved.
- If an essay takes several drafts, how can I be expected to produce a good essay in forty minutes in the exam room? Good question. Go straight to Chapter 9 if you can't wait to find out the answer!

It is a common saying that 'Writing means rewriting'. We often think that because a published, finished piece of writing seems flawless, the writer producing it was infallible. However, a finished product will have taken much rewriting: usually several drafts at least. Quite possibly the first drafts would be unrecognisable as the source of the final product.

You can write. You'll never know that until you do it.

The stages of writing

The writing process involves a series of stages. At the start of my essay-writing workshops, I always ask people their aims. The only person I've ever told I couldn't help wanted to learn to 'get it right first off'. He stayed on anyway and ended up happy enough to learn how to write like the rest of us mortals.

Depending on the stage of the essay, we tend to write in different ways:

1 The pre-writing stage

The pre-writing stage is the time between being given the question and actually starting to draft the essay. This includes organising your thoughts, reading and taking notes, 'incubating', and starting to plan your essay. ('Incubating' means letting your ideas 'hatch' over a few days or so.)

Many students assume there is only one 'right' way to answer any essay question. Essays must always be relevant but there are many different ways of answering a question; at the pre-writing stage, you plan how to answer the question. In the HSC you will often encounter essay questions that indicate in some way how to structure your answer.

The pre-writing stage is more problematic in English, however, for while you get plenty of opportunity for individual, independent thought, sometimes you are given few specific guidelines for your answer. Fortunately there are ways of preparing for this (see Chapter 7). In English it is inevitable that you will come up with a different answer to others because of a range of factors that can influence you, including:

- the way you interpret the question
- different shades of understanding of key terms
- your own background knowledge, including your cultural background
- whether you agree with a statement
- what weight you give to different aspects of the question

- additional materials you have found yourself
- the connections you make between prescribed texts, other readings and sources.

Some people call pre-writing the 'chaos' stage, since there is such a jumble of facts, thoughts, reference books, critical guides, interpretations, personal opinions and other sources available that you can get information overload, or find it hard to 'find the forest for the trees'. Since you can't cover every single aspect of a topic, you must narrow it down: on what angle, aspect or theme should you concentrate?

As you will see later, in most cases you can take particular guidance from the essay question itself.

2 First sketches and drafts

There are many reasons for finding it hard to 'get it out onto paper': apart from not being completely sure what you're trying to say, it could be nervousness, lack of self-esteem, being too hard on yourself, or telling yourself 'that's no good' or 'it'll never work' or 'that's not the right answer'. Maybe other people have given you a hard time in the past, and now you keep doing the same to yourself!

Remind yourself that the first draft is always a bit of a 'garble'. It's an experiment: feel free to push out those half-formed thoughts and vague ideas and don't worry about the words used to express them yet. No-one but you has to see your first drafts, so you are free to experiment.

In fact, many people have to get that 'garble' out of the way first; you can't start climbing the mountain from half-way up. The novelist Evelyn Waugh (*The Loved One*, *Brideshead Revisited*, and many more), when asked the secret of his style, replied something like this: 'It's simple. First I get all the words out, then I push them around a little'. In a second draft you start to 'push the words around' to make more sense.

Planning even your first draft is preferable, but even some very experienced essay writers find they can't make a plan until after that, so the 'garble' draft provides a guide to the second. If necessary, write your first draft in the spirit of brainstorming. No doubt you have used this technique elsewhere: usually in a group, everyone contributes their ideas, and all ideas are recorded without criticism, no matter how ridiculous. The whole point is to produce as many ideas as possible.

The first draft is often the hardest step to take, so don't inhibit yourself by being too self-critical. Later on, you will re-read and decide which parts to use and which not. Tell yourself you are 'prospecting' or mining for ideas, and you will come up with some valuable material among the unusable stuff. The more material you dig up, the better the chance of finding something worthwhile, and it's far better to have too much than too little to choose from.

3 Focusing

Once those first ideas are expressed, rewriting is a series of clarifications: making your ideas clearer, and more clearly expressed, by degrees—refining your 'ore'. As you sort through all the dirt and rock you've dug up, you should find some gold. Of course it doesn't emerge shining and whole from the ground, but in an imperfect state, so you need to refine it and shape it appropriately.

Reading back over what you have written, focus on the strongest points and build your essay on them.

4 Redefining/Refocusing

You may find that the draft essay needs change of some sort: perhaps you've left out important points. You may need further research, or to re-read your textbooks. You may have included discussion of facts that are irrelevant and should be taken out. The focus of attention may need to be broadened or narrowed, or perhaps you haven't answered the question properly.

Sometimes (particularly with English again) what you originally wanted to say is different from, or even the reverse of, what you now consider the best answer. That's okay: writing essays is a learning process and deliberately adopting an attitude of openness, of 'discovery' through writing, will help free you up for this.

In redefining, you check the facts, the logic and conclusions of your draft essay. Check definitions of keywords and any other areas you're not certain of.

5 Editing

The final stages of clarification and refining are the 'editing' stages. Editing means several things but a handy working definition would be 'to prepare a piece of writing to be read by the public'. In other words, to check your essay over to make it as professional and polished as possible.

Editing operates on two levels, the 'macro' and 'micro' levels. *Macro-editing* looks at the 'big picture', particularly the structure of the essay, answering the question, and the discussion of points. Is there a clear introduction and conclusion? Are the main points ordered in a logical way? Does the conclusion refer to the main points raised in the introduction? Are any important details missing? Are some of the matters discussed irrelevant to the question? Has paragraphing been used correctly throughout?

Micro-editing looks at the finer details, such as grammar, spelling and punctuation, and most of this is done at the final draft stage, polishing the essay before it is handed in. Imprecise use of language can obscure the intended meaning of your words, or even alter it. One student wrote that 'People who are both women and men play pool'. What he meant to say was that men and women play pool; what he actually said would make us wonder about the gender of the pool players!

A 'word perfect' presentation is certainly impressive in all subjects, and is a definite asset for English assignments. However, you shouldn't worry about the finer points until editing the final draft. Don't worry about spelling and grammar too much until then. Ideas, structure and facts must come first. Don't bother polishing the sculpture until the shape is complete! In the words of the great satirist Jonathan Swift:

> When a Man's Thoughts are clear, the properest Words will generally offer themselves first; and his own Judgement will direct him in what Order to place them, so as they may be best understood.

(And speaking of micro-editing, these days the word 'properest' would be changed to 'most proper', nor do we use 'Man' to stand for 'people' in general, since this is considered sexist.)

A word of warning: don't go overboard with editing. Writers can get rather neurotic and find it hard to let go of a work. I once attended a reading by a well-known Canadian author. When a student asked her at what stage she knew her manuscript was finished, she replied that she had been changing the words even as she read! There comes a point when you simply have to decide that the work is finished.

3 The good essay

What an essay isn't

Let's start with a story. It's your 17th birthday and your parents have promised that if you study hard at school they will buy you a second-hand car (this is called 'bribery'). You get up in a hurry that morning. The parents' car is parked in the driveway and you know that SOMETHING has been locked up inside the garage. You beg Mum for the key and with a smile she gives it to you. Heart pounding, you push open the door, switch on the light and see:

What is it? It's … a pile of junk. Greasy engine cogs, springs, axleshafts, body panels; there's a steering wheel … you pick it up in a state of shock and stare at the thing in disbelief. You can't help yourself; you call out 'What's this?' The parents come up behind you and when you turn around, suddenly there they are beaming proudly. You fight back the tears.

'Do you like it?' Dad asks.

'What is it?'

'A sports car of course! Good eh?'

It certainly doesn't look it.

A junk heap

'Yes', Dad says proudly. 'It's a Porsche. Needs a little work of course, but it's all there. A real goer. Happy birthday.' Gee thanks Mum and Dad. They try hard.

I once had a private student studying a topic area ('The Future'), similar to the Common module in Standard and Advanced English. Diana was trying to study for the trial exams. She was bright and articulate, an excellent public speaker, but told me she was 'failing' English in most assessments and couldn't seem to write an essay.

I asked her: what do you think about this topic? What do you think about The Future?

'I don't know'.

'What do you *think* about it?'

'I've got some notes in a folder ...' Before I could stop her she flopped the folder on the desk. 'Before you open that' I said, 'What do you *think* about The Future? What's in those notes?' She said 'I don't know. Can't remember.'

'What you've got there is a pile of junk.'

She looked at me—anger starting to show in her face.

Untogether

Diana had told me she was finding it hard to collect supplementary materials on this subject. That surprised me—there is so much on this topic in the newspapers every week.

I said 'Why? What are you looking for?'

'I don't know' she said.

That's why.

The junkpile of car parts, the pile of useless notes, the inability to find the right information: all have something in common. Or rather, they lack something in common. What they lack is structure, and without structure, little can be achieved.

Sure, the car's all there. It's just up to you to put it together the right way. Sure, the notes and clippings could be useful too—but have you ever tried to solve a jigsaw puzzle without a photograph of the picture in front of you? It's a lot harder, isn't it? Ever tried finding something when you don't know what you're looking for? That's hard too.

Teachers and overworked HSC markers don't like to have to sift through random piles of words, trying to piece together what the student's trying to say; it's your job to put it together for them.

What an essay is

An essay without an argument and an organised structure is a 'pile of junk'. SORRY!

It might help to imagine you are the Crown Prosecutor in a murder trial. The charge against the defendant is read out and you're called to present your case. You have researched the matter carefully: gathered lots of evidence, read and re-read the relevant sections of the law, and put together a case to convince judge and jury that the charge is correct.

At least, you'd better have: for in a court of law the onus of proof lies on you. Just like an essay, you must not only present all the relevant information, but also show how it 'proves' your case, by means of an **argument**: a line of discussion. And any irrelevancies will only make the 'judge' cranky.

The purpose of an essay is to establish a 'case' and prove it as fully and convincingly as possible.

Essays are monumentally difficult; that's the general opinion. Let's just demolish that belief with a shatteringly simple answer:

The essay is nothing but ideas, supported by evidence.

Before I explain this further, let's look at some different ways people have tried to write essays.

1. You have something to say. You state it. You don't know what else to write. So you just keep writing anything and hope no-one notices. Essays are just all waffle anyway!
2. You write every single thing you know about a subject: lots of details. Good; that should do it. Oh, and at the end, stick in a bit of a conclusion.
3. You get blinding flashes of inspiration, write off a lengthy draft in an hour or so, and go off to sleep. Next day when you re-read it, it's gibberish.

There are lots of other variations too, but let's stick with these three 'recipes'. The first is the 'tubular spaghetti' style of essay. It twirls around in circles, just repeating itself. It's not 'going anywhere', and it's hollow.

The second is not hollow, and it's going plenty of places. All over the place in fact; nothing is keeping it together. Fair enough for an Irish stew, but not a good recipe for essays.

The third is even messier of course, virtually alphabet soup. But it does have something important: it has an idea, maybe a few. It's trying to say something, even if the words are garbled. You can probably use the ideas to build an essay. This chapter has one main idea that I'm trying to communicate: that the essay is nothing but *ideas*, supported by *evidence*. I have made an assertion: in the following discussion I will back it up with evidence.

A definition

Various definitions of 'essay' are given in dictionaries. Two lesser-known meanings describe essays as 'experiments', or as a kind of 'judgement'. *Chambers Twentieth Century Dictionary* calls it 'an attempt: a tentative effort', a 'first draft', a 'trial' or 'experiment'. The word originally meant 'weigh' and 'try, examine'. Essays often do weigh up the evidence for and against a proposition or idea, balance the arguments and come up with a detailed assessment.

Here's a useful definition:

> An essay is a *sustained argument* developing or weighing the evidence about an idea or question, and creating a *full* and satisfying *conclusion*.

There are three key elements to this—let's look at each of them in turn.

Sustained

It's no use for a defeated marathon runner to claim victory because she was fastest in the first hundred metres. Nor can your essay come up with a quick answer and leave it at that: 'sustained' means that you keep it going. When I was in Year 11 the head teacher of English used to write at the end of my essays: 'You must write more'. My reaction was, 'Why? I've said all I wanted to in a few paragraphs, so why pad it all out into several pages?' I couldn't see the point in wasting paper and ink.

What did the teacher really mean? (If only he'd written a more complete answer himself, I wouldn't have had to work it out for myself, much later!)

The ability to write a good essay is a skill that is as important as your knowledge and ideas themselves.

Anybody can respond randomly to a 'multiple guess' test and have about one in four chances of getting the right answer. But to be able to write a whole, cohesive essay shows that you have a genuine understanding of your topic, as well as the ability to express it. Essays aren't merely about 'giving the right answer' but about demonstrating the depth and extent of your understanding and knowledge, your ability to reason, to argue an opinion, to make judgements, to analyse, to express yourself in written language fluently, and to employ appropriate terminology. Writing 'more' does *not* mean padding an essay with repetition or irrelevant details, 'telling the story' or using random quotes, etc. Padding is extremely easy to spot, and most unimpressive to the marker!

Argument (line of discussion)

Forget your usual understanding of the word 'argument': the essay isn't a quarrel or fight but an opinion, a proposition, an idea, a theme or the disclosure of information. The word 'argument' is used in this book to mean your main line of discussion, the theme you are developing. Arguments are the backbone of the essay.

An essay, like a tree, can grow from one simple source. A tree can begin with one seed. This germinates and sprouts, sending the first shoots out into the light of day. Properly nurtured, with appropriate nutrients and conditions, that thin stem will eventually grow into a tall, thick trunk.

Your essay can grow on paper, under the study lamp, from one single idea—your argument or theme—and should develop in a straight line from start to finish (otherwise it has problems).

The analogy can be extended further: a tree can be very complex, having many branches, sub-branches, leaves, etc. It may flower, fruit, and even harbour various inhabitants! But always that main structure is there. Likewise, your argument may branch off into various topics, but these must be linked somehow to the argument (otherwise they'll fall off!). Of course, these branches can have sub-branches and small details themselves.

Full conclusion

In the best essays, conclusions 'bear fruit': they go beyond a mere summary of the discussion and look at the implications and significance more fully.

There's our definition of the essay: it's not merely an idea, but is one line of discussion supported by information and knowledge, pruned and nurtured by your writing and editing skills. The best essays cap off the discussion with some sense of 'something extra': what the discussion leads us to conclude, the implications of what we have written. (*Note*: The conclusion should not, however, introduce new material.)

The good essay

What makes a good essay? The good essay is:

- relevant
- complete
- cohesive
- sustained
- well organised
- concise
- 'signposted'
- specific
- explanatory
- analytical/critical
- fluently expressed.

Each of these terms is now explained briefly. In Chapter 4 they are treated in more detail and exercises are given to help you practise relevant skills.

Relevant

Answer the question! It is *not* good enough to write just anything about the general subject; you must meet the specific requirements. This shouldn't need to be said at all, but an overwhelming number of teachers agree: one of the most common errors made by students is simply not answering the question. There are a number of possible ways this could happen:

- You can't understand the question.
- You can't analyse the question.
- You don't have any answer.
- You don't know much about the topic.
- You haven't bothered to try!

If your problem is either of the first two, help is at hand in Chapter 4. The more experience you get with answering questions, the better you'll become at understanding them and learning to know the kinds of questions to expect. If it's either of the next two, you need to work on your study. If your problem is the last alternative, I must emphasise that it is far less 'bother' to consider the question from the start than to go off on a detour and have to start all over again later!

Open questions and closed questions

Essay questions can offer a varied scope of response, from 'open' to 'closed'. The *open* question is broad and allows many options in your answer. A good example of an open type is this HSC English question:

> How have the texts you have studied this year effectively shaped your understanding of the meaning of 'change'? In your answer you should refer to your prescribed text, ONE text from the prescribed stimulus booklet *Changing*, and a variety of other related texts of your own choosing.
>
> Source: BOSTES NSW 2001 Higher School Certificate Specimen Examination Paper, English (Standard) and (Advanced)

This question does specify the theme of change, but otherwise allows you a free hand in deciding what aspects to discuss, so long as you refer to the variety of texts they stipulate and answer how these texts have 'effectively shaped' your understanding.

Open questions give you much freedom, and for students who are well prepared, they can be a godsend. On the other hand, they may give you little direction, and that is why many students flounder on such questions; unable to think of anything, not knowing where to start.

Many students believe that a *closed* question is easier because it 'tells you what to do'. It specifies more narrowly the aspects of a topic on which you should focus. A closed question on a novel might ask you to discuss the relationship of two main characters, a particular incident in relation to the whole story, a quote or a particular theme. Here is an example of a 'closed' essay question:

> Australia is a limited market. Businesses situated in such markets seek global remedies. Critically examine how the Australian market is limiting the growth of a business you have studied and the consequences for two different stakeholders when this business expands into the global marketplace.
>
> Source: BOSTES NSW, 2001 HSC Specimen Examination Paper, Business Studies

The above question requires you to understand what is meant by a 'limited market', to know about 'global remedies', how the Australian market has limited the growth of a business you have studied, and the consequences of global expansion.

Both kinds of question have their pros and cons. The freedom of the 'open' question must be met with your own initiative, but at least it gives you more scope to write about what interests you, or what you have studied and thought about most closely. While the closed question does signpost the way for you, it could be a way with which you're not very familiar: a technical aspect of theatre, film or multimedia, a minor character, an unexpected theme or aspect, or something you've simply overlooked or ignored.

Either way, you still have to make sure to answer the question!

Complete

'Complete' doesn't mean long, nor filled with irrelevant details. It certainly doesn't mean 'containing every single fact you know about the topic' either. A complete essay has an argument, discussion of a number of points relating to that, and a conclusion tying the points together. It doesn't assume that the reader already knows what they need to know; the complete essay discusses all that is necessary to establish your point and includes all the logical steps to build up the whole picture.

Cohesive

'Cohesive' means that it 'hangs together'. What we are reading isn't a random set of facts, or just a pile of words, but points with a definite purpose in common.

Sustained

This purpose is *sustained* throughout the essay.

Well organised

A well-organised essay is structured so that related points are grouped together and so that there's a logic to their sequence (that is, we can see how each point leads to the next). A well-organised essay introduces the main points early and then treats each of them in turn, according to some logical order.

Concise (and clear)

Don't be unnecessarily wordy. Your meaning is often clearer when it's expressed in fewer words. Some students will take four or five lines to express an idea that needs only two.

'Signposted'

It is very annoying to read some interesting discussion, and yet be unable to see what the writer is actually getting at. You can 'show the way' to a reader by:

- announcing your points in advance
- using linking words and phrases
- showing how your points relate to the main theme
- using sequence words, such as 'firstly', 'secondly', etc.

Specific

It is always impressive to see that a writer is closely engaged with the subject material: it is advisable to quote relevant details about events or theories and to use the appropriate technical terminology or specialised vocabulary in support of your argument. In English, a specific essay will discuss significant characters or scenes in detail. In Economics, quote financial events, policy changes, statistics, etc.

You may know a lot about a subject but if you don't get specific, you haven't 'proved' this, and you've undersold yourself. Your reader is not a mindreader!

Explanatory

It's one thing to know your facts but another to be able to explain their significance—obviously it is preferable to 'prove' your case by making explicit links between facts you introduce and your argument.

Advanced essay skills

Analysis

An average student might take ideas found in books for granted, at their 'face value'. Better-than-average students look deeper.

Fluency

In English in particular, the top-banded essays are very well expressed. This takes practice!

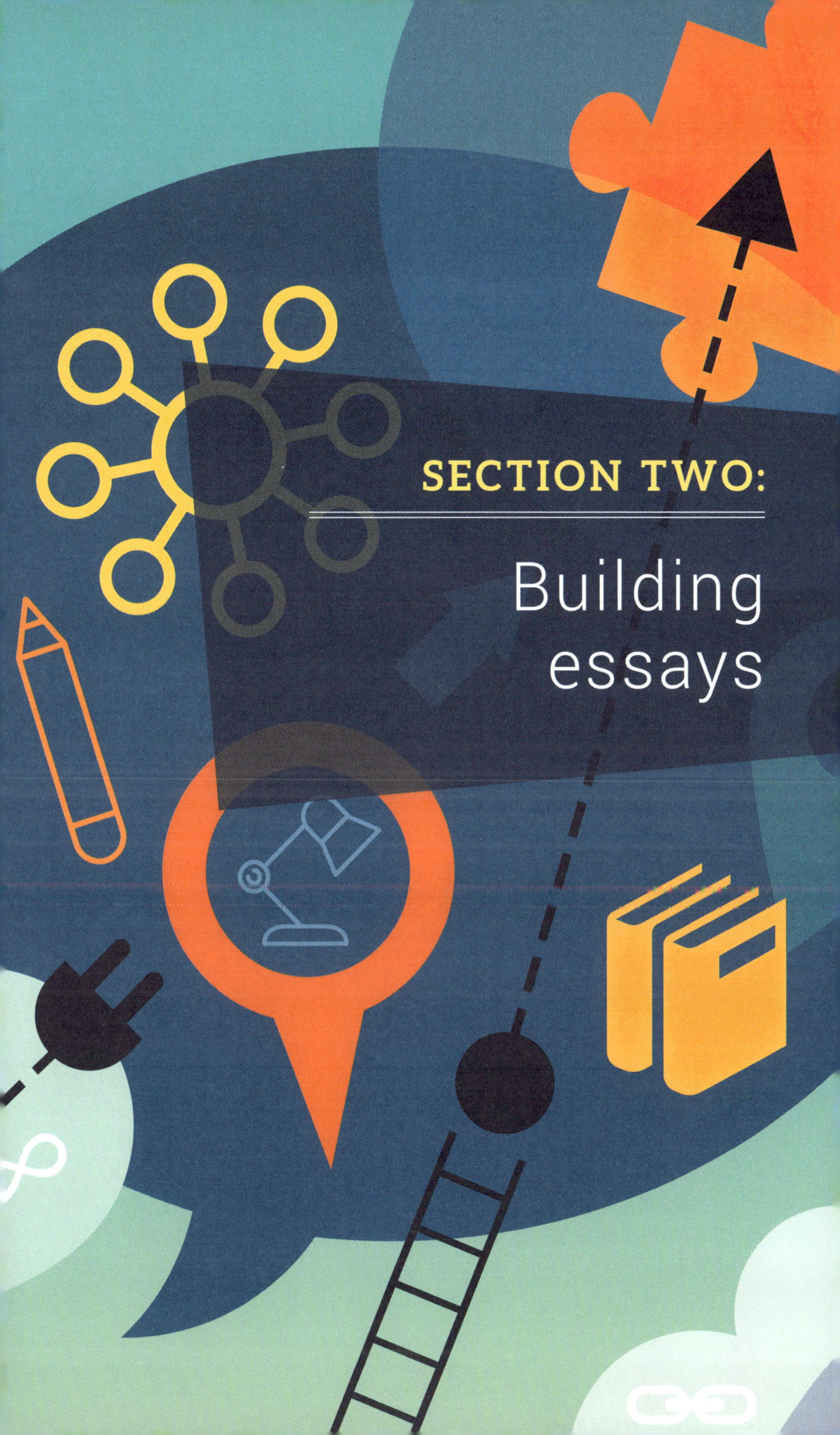

SECTION TWO:

Building essays

4 Training workouts: the microskills

Analysing the question: relevant

What is the question really about? What is it asking you to do? Analysing the question is crucial: it's rather tragic for students who hand in a fine essay on the right subject, only to discover that they didn't answer the question. This goes down very poorly with teachers and examiners! One way of making sure you're 'on track' is to note carefully the keywords.

Find keywords

Keywords are the clues in a question that specify the subject you are to discuss, refer you to a particular aspect of it, and tell you what to do in your discussion.

- *Subject* keywords tell you what text or broad area of study you are to discuss. These may be specified in a heading above the question itself in HSC papers, but may not be in class essays. (You are not likely to get this wrong, most of the time!)
- *Topic* keywords specify what part of the subject you should discuss.
- *Aspect* keywords specify that particular parts of that topic be considered.
- '*Doing*' keywords specify what you are asked to 'do'; for example, 'explain', 'discuss', 'compare', etc.

Discuss a range of strategies that could be used by employers in the business services industry to raise employee awareness of issues relating to occupational health and safety.

Source: BOSTES NSW 2001 HSC Specimen Examination Paper, Business Services—Office Administration

In the above question, the broad *subject* is the business services industry. The specific focus or *topic* is occupational health and safety. The *aspect* of that focus you are asked about is strategies to raise employee awareness, and the '*doing*' keyword is to 'discuss'.

Any question will have keywords, although you may not find all four types. For example, a question may specify a broad topic related to the subject but leave the choice of particular aspects up to you.

EXERCISES

1 Look up old exam papers in the subjects you are studying and find the keywords in essay questions.

2 Decide the type of each keyword.

The 3-step structure: complete

The essay has a simple 1–2–3 structure. A similar pattern can also be used in a paragraph. It's excellent practice—a kind of 'micro-essay'.

In one paragraph we can announce a 'case', support it and then cap it off in some way. I use three simple terms to help remind me of what I'm trying to achieve:

Guess what? | Prove it! | So what?

- *Guess what?*—What am I trying to say, establish, describe or prove? This is stated in a topic sentence. (We look at topic sentences in the next section. They form the backbone of the paragraph, just as the argument is the backbone of an essay.)
- *Prove it!*—How can I back it up?
- *So what?*—Try to 'make something of it'. Relate this to my main argument or cap off the point I'm making here.

EXERCISES

Read the following paragraph carefully and relate each section to the above steps.

1. Energy conservation is an environmental issue with implications for everyday life. 2. In their own homes, people have the choice to reduce their energy consumption by various means: by cutting down on unnecessary energy consumption, by installing insulation, by designing energy-efficient homes such as 'solar passive', and by using 'green' energy sources such as solar energy. 3. Not to conserve energy in the household is to choose not to care about the environment.

Now read the following three paragraphs and decide whether or not they follow this pattern. Where does each step begin?

A The poems of Bruce Dawe are preoccupied with the suburban life of Australia. In particular, 'Enter without so much as knocking', 'Homo Suburbiensis', 'Life cycle' and 'And a Good Friday was had by all' treat various aspects of suburban life, such as the corrupting influence of consumerism, the meaningless chatter of the commercial media, the snatches of trivial conversation. However, not all is lost: in 'Homo Suburbiensis' the gardener has found in his suburban patch an oasis of quiet in which to contemplate the timeless issues of 'pain, love, hate, age, war, death, laughter, fever.'

B In this essay I will outline some of the areas that have benefited from changing values and norms in relation to the family, focusing on Australian families. First I will look at the functions performed by the family, and how the structure of the family has evolved from an extended kin family to an isolated nuclear family. Then I will look at the changes in reasons for marriage and the reasons for staying married, showing that now romantic love is the motivation for marriage, as opposed to economic benefit. Finally I will outline how many of the changes in values and norms in relation to the family have benefited women and children.

C Writing is a craft, and like many crafts it requires a variety of skills. The leather worker may need a steady hand, a straight eye, and an appreciation of quality materials, as well as a creative flair for embossing designs and choosing appropriate buckles, etc. The essay writer must develop a variety of skills too: these include efficient study or research, clear thinking, the ability to use an appropriate form, and the ability to use language persuasively and correctly. The isolation of these particular skills also makes it possible to identify and work on individual areas of weakness.

ANSWERS TO EXERCISES

a Yes.

1 'The poems of ...'

2 'In particular, ...'

3 'Not all is lost ...'

b No.

1 'In this essay I will ...'

2 'First I will look ...'

(This is obviously an introductory paragraph, and a final 'cap' is not required here.)

c Yes.

1 'Writing is a craft ...'

'... requires a variety of skills ...'

2 'The leather worker ...'

'The essay writer ...'

3 'The isolation of ...'

(This is a more complicated example because it is 'double-barrelled': the writer is making a comparison throughout, between crafts and writing.)

Completeness in short-response answers

I had a student who asked me why he only got half a mark out of two for a reading passage question. The question asked something like 'How does the writer feel?', and John had written: 'She feels sad'. 'That's right isn't it?' he asked.

Yes, it was right. But those few words weren't worth two marks. A complete answer will tell us quite a bit more than he did. The reading passage was a newspaper feature article written by a mother, about her daughter leaving home. We can follow the 1-2-3 pattern:

- *Guess what?*—The mother is sad.

The next step is to 'Prove it'. A relevant quote will help.

- *Prove it*—'The page is swimming before her eyes': in other words, she's crying.

Now we can cap this off in some way. The obvious way would be to explain why she's sad.

- *So what?*—'She's crying because just when her daughter's old enough to be her friend, she's losing her to the daughter's own friends.'

EXERCISES

Write complete paragraphs using the '3-step pattern', starting with the following:

1 There are many reasons for introducing daylight saving.
2 It's wrong to say that essay-writing skills are important; they are essential!
3 Before criticising his friend's faults, he should have looked at his own first.
4 There are many exciting things to do on Slipstream Island.
5 It was a perfect day.

Topic sentences: cohesive

A very common and important student weakness is the lack of topic sentences. Topic sentences:

- give shape and purpose to your writing
- help create order within the paragraph
- allow the reader to follow the argument
- demonstrate an understanding of formal writing.

The topic sentence often, but not always, begins the paragraph and states or introduces the *theme* of that paragraph or the point it's making. (However, it will sometimes appear at the end of a paragraph and sometimes in the middle. There is no rule about this.) To start a paragraph with a topic sentence is to start with a purpose, and while it gives the paragraph unity and order, it also gives power to your writing by focusing it.

If you are asked to write a paragraph about the characters in a particular drama or novel, it's human nature to start just listing them in no particular order, briefly describing them according to whatever ideas first come to mind. Writing a topic sentence 'up front' will help convert 'junk' into building blocks.

About Peter Skrzynecki's poem 'Migrant Hostel' you could say that:

> The poem describes the migrants as birds, or like imprisoned criminals, or like helpless dumb creatures.

These points may be correct, but the sentence reads like an unconvincing list of ideas, which doesn't really tell us much. The following paragraph develops one idea, stated in a topic sentence at the start:

> Stanza by stanza, Skrzynecki builds up an image of helpless, caged birds. Initially described as people who can't keep track of what's going on, the migrants are then compared to a homing pigeon 'circling to get its bearings'. These birds, however, aren't really 'homing' because they have left home, and in the third stanza they are more like 'birds of passage' but without the freedom to follow the seasons at their will. Finally the barricading arm of the migrant hostel completes the effect of their being imprisoned; these people's lives are either effectively behind them now, or they are helplessly waiting for their life to begin.

In the above paragraph, the strongest idea has been selected and the rest of the paragraph develops the idea stated in the topic sentence.

Topic sentences make your writing easier to read and your argument easier to follow. More importantly, they ensure that you are clear about what *you* are trying to say. As an exercise, make a point when revising your essays of highlighting the topic sentence in each paragraph. If you can't find one, write one for it. (This may also involve reshaping the entire paragraph; your work will be stronger for the extra effort.)

EXERCISES

Recognising topic sentences

Read the following paragraphs and decide whether they have topic sentences or not. If so, underline them.

1 When I arrived at university I found that I could no longer expect everyone and everything to change for my sake. In fact, it was me who had to change. Not everyone agreed with my opinions in tutorials. Not everyone felt I was an outstanding fount of wisdom. From being a class leader at school, I was now just one of the group, no more special than anyone else.

2 You can go to the beach or for a long hike in the bush. How about a long bike ride or hiring a tennis court for the afternoon with a group of friends? Then there are less energetic activities too: why not catch a new movie or visit the art gallery? Learn a new craft, or how to play an instrument? There are always plenty of things to do in your holidays.

3 Opinions about Madonna are divided. Some women feel that she has been a very positive symbol of female pride and strength, since she projects such a confident, self-assured image and seems to know exactly what she wants and how to get it. Others complain that her emphasis on body image and fashion just reinforces the old male myth that women are just sex objects.

4 *The Club* is a drama about the politics of an Aussie Rules football club, but really this could be the story of any sporting organisation. An old club tradition is betrayed by 'buying' the star player Geoff Hayward. Jock, the club's administrator, pretends to be a father figure to Geoff but then betrays his confidence. And the coach Laurie is betrayed by the entire club, although they feel he betrayed them by making comments to the media.

ANSWERS TO EXERCISES

1 first sentence

2 last sentence

3 first sentence

4 Trick: the first sentence appears to be a topic sentence, yet close reading shows that the student hasn't actually written about this topic at all.
A better topic sentence would focus on 'betrayal' as a theme.

Composing topic sentences

Here is a series of paragraphs, with the topic sentences removed. Try to make up a topic sentence to go with them.

1 ... If you don't have a passport, you must apply for one well in advance of your departure. Many countries require an entry visa. Travel insurance is also considered an absolute necessity. And if you are planning to drive overseas, you must apply for an international driving permit in some countries.

2 There will be women reading this book who may well be saying to themselves, 'This is all very well and good, but it's hardly of interest to me. What chance do I have of ever becoming Prime Minister?' The answer is that your chances are better than you think and a lot better than they would have been twenty or even ten years ago ... As the following tables will show, the number of women MPs is increasing annually. The more female MPs there are, the more chance there is of one of them getting into The Lodge. Where once there was a reluctance by political parties to endorse women as candidates, there is now keen competition between parties to have the most women in the various parliaments.

Source: Cohen, B 1990, *How to Become Prime Minister*, Ringwood, Penguin, p. 76

3 ... They sing in the air, buzz in the classrooms, wail in streets, murmur in bedrooms. They shape daily lives and nightly fears. Wars are begun on the strength of a good story and could not be started without one. If a people's stories are destroyed they wander dispossessed on the fringes of others' stories, and eventually dissolve into oblivion. Journeys are begun, colonies are founded, hearts are broken, souls inspired. If you're not in a story, you don't exist ...

Source: Miller, P 1997, *The Last One Who Remembers*, Sydney, Allen and Unwin, p. 17

4 There are no prizes for getting it right. There was no moment when, for the first time, Australia was seen 'as it really was' ... A national identity is an invention. There is no point asking whether one version of this essential Australia is truer than another because they are all intellectual constructs, neat, tidy, comprehensible—and necessarily false. They have all been artificially imposed upon a diverse landscape and population, and a variety of untidy social relationships, attitudes and emotions.

Source: White, R 1981, *Inventing Australia*, Sydney, Allen and Unwin, p. viii

ANSWERS TO EXERCISES

Your topic sentences should state something like the following:

1 There is much preparation required before travelling overseas.

2 Women's chances of becoming the Australian Prime Minister are getting better and better. (This is a very cohesive paragraph.)

3 Story is all-important.

4 There is no single, 'true' Australian identity.

Paragraphing: sustained

Paragraphing is not such a difficult skill but it is an important one. Dividing up your writing into paragraphs shows that you are organised and makes an essay easier to read. When we read an essay we want to see how the argument is progressing from one point to the next.

Unlike this book, and unlike reports, essays don't use headings. This makes them look less 'reader friendly', so it is important to use paragraphs regularly, to break up the mass of words and to signal the making of a new point. It also tends to put the marker in a better mood! An unparagraphed page gives the reader the feeling of hacking a way through thick jungle without a track in sight—not very enjoyable, and very hard work. A neat series of paragraphs acts like stepping stones that can be followed pleasurably across the river.

Most students find the process of deciding where to begin and end paragraphs reasonably easy; you will soon get a feel for it with a little practice. Obviously, whenever you write a topic sentence, this may be a good place to start a new paragraph.

Paragraph unity

If topic sentences remind us to keep to the point, paragraphing reminds us to separate point from point, to show where one topic ends and the next begins. 'Paragraph unity' means that each paragraph deals with one main idea only. Once that point has been made and supported, move on to a new paragraph.

The topic sentence of each paragraph should propel your argument by advancing the next logical step and showing how it relates. For example, a student writing an essay about factors affecting employment patterns in Australia treated four factors:

(a) the economic climate (boom or bust?)
(b) industry restructuring
(c) privatisation and corporatisation of industries
(d) technological innovation.

She treated each of these points for a couple of paragraphs or so. The topic sentences introducing each point began like this:

(a) Traditionally the level of growth and activity of the Australian economy has been considered the chief factor affecting employment …
(b) However, with major changes in regulatory frameworks, another important factor in Australian employment patterns in recent years has been the major changes brought about by industry restructuring …
(c) Another factor affecting these patterns in recent times has been the trend to privatisation or corporatisation of functions formerly undertaken by government agencies, such as …
(d) The climate of rapid and widespread technological innovation has also had a dramatic effect on employment patterns …

Note that each sentence introduces the new point, and also reminds us of the main topic. This keeps the argument *sustained* throughout the essay.

How long should a paragraph be? There is no ideal or 'correct' length for paragraphs, although the preference is for shorter rather than longer ones. As a rough guide, consider 6–7 typed or handwritten lines a fair aim; half a page is certainly too long; three lines usually too short! The most important thing is simply to use paragraphing.

Indenting

Many teachers still prefer you to indent the start of a paragraph: that is, to start your paragraph about one tab stop to the right of the margin, or roughly one centimetre on a handwritten page. If you do start paragraphs 'flush left', that is, at the margin, like the rest of your lines, you must leave a line space between each paragraph to signal the start of a new paragraph. Check with your teacher what they prefer!

EXERCISE

Read the following extract, which has been retyped without paragraphing. Decide where paragraphs should go.

In the beginning was the pun

... Puns have always been known, and some have achieved great fame—notably the *Peter/rock* play on words in the New Testament (clearer in French, where *pierre* is used for both), or the puns used by the oracle at Delphi (such as the ambiguous reply to the general who wished to know whether he should go on a journey: *Domine, stes* vs *Domin ne stes*, 'Master, stay' vs 'At home do not stay'. Shakespeare was one of the greatest users of puns. In France, one of the most famous punsters was the Marquis de Bièvre, in whose never-acted play *Vercingétorix* there is an italicised pun in every line. Puns are a feature of many linguistic contexts, such as black comedy, sick humour, T-shirts, lapel badges, car stickers, trade names, book titles and graffiti. The world of advertising makes great use of the economical impact and freshness of a pun (e.g. the slogan for a new kind of adhesive: 'Our word is your bond'). But the best and worst of them are found in everyday conversation. Puns that have been justly lauded include the response of the disappointed recipient of poor-quality flowers ('With fronds like these who needs anemones?'), the comment made by the circus manager to the human cannonball who wanted to leave ('Where will I find another man of your calibre?'), and the comment about the Spanish girls in a certain town, that they are 'senoreaters'. Puns have been called verbal practical jokes, and are either loved or hated according to temperament. Their popularity varies greatly between languages and cultures, though the reasons for this are unclear; it has been said, for example, that they are far more popular in Britain than in the USA, and in France than in Germany. But punning is not without its dangers. The Gnat, in Lewis Carroll's *The Hunting of the Snark*, dies of a pun. And punsters should beware the phenomenon of compulsive punning, first recorded by a German surgeon in 1939, and now known as 'Förster's syndrome'.

Source: Crystal, D 1987, *The Cambridge Encyclopaedia of Language*, Cambridge, CUP, p. 63

ANSWERS

There are three paragraphs, based on three different topics introduced by the following topic sentences:

- ... Puns have always been known, and some have achieved great fame ...
- Puns are a feature of many linguistic contexts ...
- Puns have been called verbal practical jokes ...

Did you notice how hard it was to read when not paragraphed?

Organising data: well organised

Writing is very slow and *linear*: it can only travel in a straight *line*, handling one idea, one direction at a time. So it is important to unravel your ideas one by one, in an organised way. If you don't do this, your reader will become confused.

Your essay needs several levels of organisation. Firstly there is the overall Introduction–Body–Conclusion structure, which you know. Secondly you need to order the topics discussed in the body; and thirdly, within each topic, related points should be organised too.

Consider that pile of car parts again. Each individual piece belongs with specific others, and together they make up a structure called an 'assembly'. For example, steering-related parts make up a steering assembly, brake parts form a brake assembly, and so on.

Likewise, your information should be sorted into groups. This involves two main processes: *grouping* related points together, and *ranking* points within the group.

Grouping

Say you're writing an essay about *Huckleberry Finn*. Some perspectives to consider would include themes such as freedom, physical journeys, and growth of self-understanding through experience. While taking notes for the essay, you would collect information under those headings. Taking notes and organising your ideas for an Ancient History question on historical methodology, you might use the headings of written evidence, archaeology and science.

Subgrouping

You can also use subgroups where appropriate, dividing groups into smaller groups. For example, you might want to discuss 'freedom' in *Huckleberry Finn* under three different subheadings: the question of slave emancipation, the freedom of a young boy not wanting to be 'sivilised' and lead a boring life, and the freedom to decide right from wrong.

Ordering

It is important to discuss points in order. There are various ways of deciding how to arrange this, and you'll usually find that the particular essay you are writing will suggest how to do it. Different *ordering principles* are available to you:

- *Order of importance*: start with the most important or persuasive facts, then treat progressively less important ones. Or start with lesser points and work up to the most important ones. An essay about the characters in Macbeth will probably concentrate on the main characters first: Duncan, Macbeth, Lady Macbeth, etc., unless the question asks you to focus on the lesser characters.
- *From central to less central*: broad view to specific. It is conventional to give the 'big picture' before treating details. For instance, the introduction should mention the main points to be treated, but not go into detail.
- *Chronological (time) order*: A history essay might discuss events and movements in the sequence in which they occurred in time.
- *Geography*: you could describe the terrain of a country, starting from west and working east, then from north to south, etc. You could describe a house starting from (say) the exterior, then moving to the interior, then going from room to room, starting from the front.
- *Cause–effect*: this is the idea that something caused an effect of some sort. To answer why Ted is led to resigning as Club President in David Williamson's play *The Club*, you need to trace the causes in the events preceding it. Sometimes there may be a *causal chain*, where a series of events is set off by some factor.
- *Comparison*: you can discuss all the positive aspects first, then the negative (or vice versa), e.g., the advantages and disadvantages of a government policy.

EXERCISES

1 **a** Think about the English text you have read or viewed most recently. (A 'text' can also include a film or multimedia production.) Make a list of the characters according to three categories:

- main characters
- minor characters
- incidental characters (people who only make a brief, passing appearance).

b Make a similar list of major, minor and trivial incidents in that book.

2 **a** What is important to you in your life? Think of at least four categories of things that are important to you. Use these categories as headings and list five examples under each heading.

b For each category, give each of these five examples a number from 1 to 5, starting with the most important.

3 Look at the above list of organisational principles. Think of an essay topic where you might use each one. In which subjects might you use them? e.g., Modern History, Legal Studies, Earth and Environmental Science

4 Think of a recent event. What was the cause (or causes), in your opinion? Make a list of everything that might have contributed to this happening. For example:

Causes of events in Ron's household that night

- Ron had a stressful day at work.
- He had to stay back late to fix an emergency problem, so missed his usual train home.
- He missed the last bus from the station, and had to walk.
- He hates being late.
- He arrived home very late, angry and tired.
- Ron snapped at his kids when they greeted him.
- Ron apologised to his kids.

Summarising: concise

Summarising is an essential skill, for the following reasons:

Getting the big picture

Before treating details, we first need to understand the overall situation. As we've discussed, it's hard to finish a jigsaw without knowing what the picture looks like. Most novels, for instance, will be composed of a number of characters and a series of events or other developments. *The Stolen Children* tells many different stories in one book, but we need to be able to discuss the book as a whole.

Simplifying your notes and ideas

Another word for summary is *precis*, and a good summary is both precise and concise since it decides what are the essential points, and what are the lesser, supporting points.

Articulating your ideas

Writing a summary makes you express your ideas on paper, to test and develop them. Often we believe we know what we feel about a film or book until we actually try to find words to express this. Students tend to assume that summarising is more or less 'automatic', and yet when asked to summarise an English text, they just start to 'tell the story' from the beginning, or to recount whatever they can remember.

That is not a 'summary', however. Some people can rattle off the entire story of a movie in vivid detail, scene by scene, yet are completely unable to encapsulate what it's 'all about', to give the gist of it quickly. That's what we do need: a general overview. Frequently we discover that we have to give the matter further thought. A short summary can be an excellent foundation for all further study in a topic, since it starts the process of clarifying your thoughts at an early stage.

Helping you remember

Summaries help to cement important ideas in your memory. The best way to remember things is to actively organise your thoughts in some way. It's an excellent idea to summarise a book or topic immediately after studying it, so that you don't forget most of it months later, as so many students do.

A summary gives you the 'big picture' in few words!

The idea of a summary is to reduce a complex set of information to a manageable whole. The length can vary, but you may discover that the smaller the summary, the harder it is to write. So this is a great exercise in concision. Try, for instance, to write a one-paragraph summary of the last book you have read. Here are some pointers:

Give the essential information: Who, what, where, when, how and why. About Michael Gow's play *Away*, we could say that 'The drama is set in Australia in the summer holidays of 1967–68, and focuses on the problems and aspirations of three separate family groups.' We could go on to outline these separate problems and aspirations, probably starting with the sickness of Harry and Vic's son, Tom. It can take a little practice to see which points are essential and which aren't. The best test is to try to eliminate them: if the summary still makes sense, the detail isn't necessary.

Just as the essay is structured 1–2–3, and just as the paragraph and short response exam answer can follow this pattern, so can the summary.

Here is the beginning of a three-step summary of Bruce Dawe's poem 'Abandonment of Autos'. The first step is to sum up broadly. Then we start to add detail.

1 This is a poem inspired by the attraction of freedom.

2 It focuses on the freedom of abandoning a car, rather than going through the usual process of trade-ins or of getting an evaluation from the wrecker.

In this section we have introduced our idea, and then expanded on it. We can either continue to support this idea with more detail, or proceed to 'cap it off' by some means.

3 However, the poem is more meaningful when considered as an allegory for general freedom in life, rather than an apparently whimsical story.

Or:

Beyond this trivial story lies a message about the importance of individualism and making up your own mind about things.

Or:

Dawe uses this theme to stress the importance of valuing everyday items less casually, using our freedom of thought to find meaning even in small matters.

It may concern you that a summary seems to oversimplify. However, in the body of the essay you will get an opportunity to expand on, clarify and qualify your points; to discuss details in all their complexity.

A good summary will:

- *define* your understanding of the book or topic
- *introduce* the major points
- *interpret* it—that is, 'make something of it'.

Summary writing, like most essay-writing skills, improves with practice.

EXERCISES

1. Choose whichever English text you have read or seen most recently. Write *no more* than three paragraphs summarising the main theme(s), main characters and situation. Use the 1–2–3 pattern.
2. Do this for every other English text you are studying. (Keep these exercises with your notes on that text, as they are useful study exercises.)
3. Summarise your understanding of a topic area in another subject such as Economics, Legal Studies or Geography. Some clues: What are the main points we need to know about that topic? What are the key terms, key facts, theories or issues?

Linking: 'signposted'

'Signposting' your argument makes a favourable impression, since it shows not only that you're organised but that you're courteously considering your reader as well. It's a common experience to settle into reading an essay and then find that one seems to have 'lost the plot' of what the writer is saying. Probably the writer has changed the topic but forgotten to tell the reader this. Signals need to be 'planted' into the next draft.

Using linking words and phrases helps to reinforce your essay by 'welding' the parts together. The actual words you need to use will be suggested by what you are saying. Here are some examples of connectives—ways of linking ideas:

Linking words

also	however
afterwards	subsequently
consequently	therefore
yet	meanwhile
moreover	thus

Linking phrases

as a result of this
some time later
a more significant factor
a fourth concern
for example

Linking between paragraphs

- *Numbering*: 'Firstly we must consider the question of … Secondly we must look at …'
- *Chronological*: (sequence of events) 'Some time after this first eruption of violence, policy changes began to be considered …'
- *Contrast*: 'An even more important factor is …'

'The opposite viewpoint is discussed by Adam Smith, who claims that …'

- *Cause/effect*: 'Because of this, the following changes were soon implemented …'
- *Adding*: 'Another example of this phenomenon is …'
- *Comparing*: 'A similar event was the case of Hutchinson Bros, a firm which …'
- *Summarising*: 'Therefore there is little narrative interest in this novel. However, the opposite is the case in *Huckleberry Finn* …'

EXERCISES

1. Look at any page of writing in a textbook and find as many linking words and phrases as you can.
2. Use linking words or phrases to join these sentences into one sentence.

   a There is nothing illegal about this.
   I am not perfectly happy about it.

   b I was walking down the street.
   I saw Natasha.

   c What are you going to do?
   Your casual job has finished.

   d My money is all gone.
   I will learn how to save in future.

   e Your theory is debatable.
   One could argue for or against it.

Quoting: specific

Your essay gives an opportunity to show what you know about the topic, and getting specific and detailed is a means of doing so. There are two quoting skills worth focusing on here:

- quoting details
- direct quotes.

Quoting details

A well-organised essay takes us on a journey, from the broad *overview* of the introduction, breaking it down to general *topics*, and then in the body of the essay, getting down to specific *detail*.

Say you wanted to write an essay about Louis Nowra's play *Così*, focusing on 'perspective'. This play is about a young man fresh out of university, directing his first play in an institution for the mentally ill, in 1971. At the *overview* level, you could say that some key themes are the following: conflicting perspectives, madness and sanity, art and reality. At the *topic* level, we look at various kinds of perspective, various forms of madness and sanity, and various representations of art and reality. At the *detail* level we discuss each topic in relation to particular people, scenes, themes and incidents, and so on.

The diagram on page 47 illustrates these three levels, concentrating on the 'perspective' strand only.

In this diagram you can see that we start with an overview of the themes of the work as a whole and then analyse the various strands of each theme, such as 'perspective', before getting even more detailed.

Many students restrict most of their discussion to the first two levels, which has two negative effects: you seem either not to be interested in the work very much or not to know much more than the general picture. To quote details is far more impressive than running out of things to say, and just repeating vague generalities such as:

> 'Perspective is how you look at things' or 'Different people have different perspectives', and so on.

The next time you get stuck, start discussing more details: quote scenes or lines, incidents or uses of language that back up your statements and help you to develop your argument further.

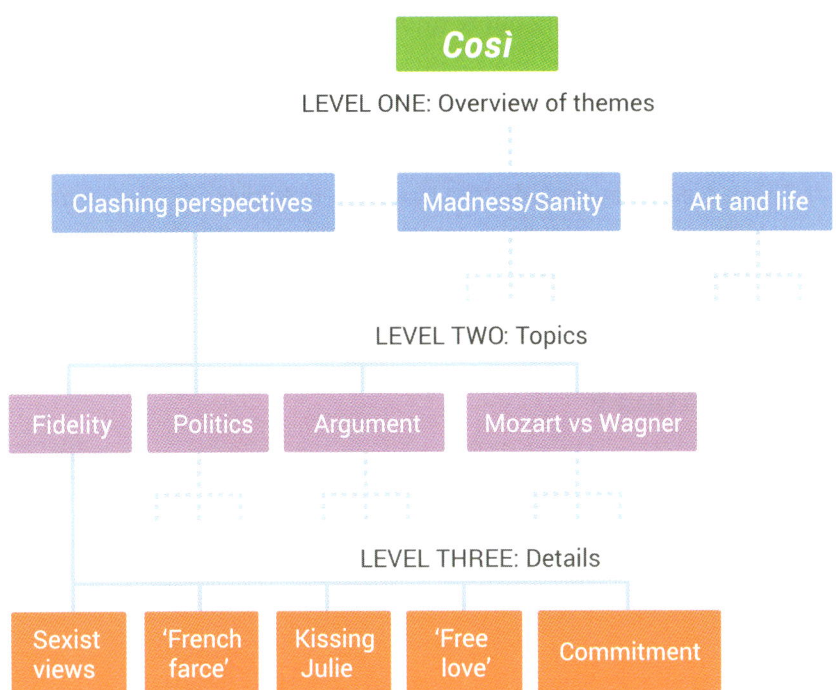

Direct quoting

Quoting from books, from film dialogue or from speech is not one of the more difficult skills, but it is unimpressive when attention hasn't been paid to the rules:

- If quoting speech, put the actual speech (only) within inverted commas. Eric said: 'Please come immediately. My car won't start'.
- You can quote relevant authors by introducing them with phrases like: 'According to Jean Quirk ...', or 'It is the opinion of James Brown that ...'
- Do not change the actual wording *at all*. And check that you've written it 'word for word': it is very bad to misquote a professional writer, especially in English. In exams, you are not expected to remember long quotes word for word. It is better to paraphrase your quotes. For example, write the following: Melvyn Bragg says words to the effect that ' ... '
- You *can* leave words out, where this part of the quote is irrelevant to your argument, and it is preferable to do so. Use an *ellipsis* (set of three dots). Tamara said 'For goodness' sake ... please get more organised'. (Make your own guesses about what she might have said in-between!)
- If you do have to change the wording to fit in with your sentence, make this clear by putting the changed words in square brackets: Tamara said that '[we] couldn't organise a paper chase in a newsagency!'

- Finally you can put a long quote (more than 2–3 lines) in a special indented block, like this:

> A word of warning: don't become a 'quote specialist' who tries to cobble an entire essay together from a string of quotes without an argument. These are sometimes referred to as 'straw essays'. Quotes alone will not 'prove' your point: details must be related to an argument; arguments must be supported by details. Once you have quoted something, you should explain how this relates to your argument.

EXERCISES

1. Describe a recent holiday you had. First give an overview, then list topics, then describe actual details in support.
2. You are writing an essay about alcoholism, and have just quoted the following sentence from a reference book: 'Alcoholism is not merely a disease, but a major social problem'. Continue the discussion for a paragraph or two, explaining how this supports your argument about how alcoholism should be treated. (Improvise details, if necessary, for the purposes of this exercise.)

Explaining

Not only should you reveal details and facts, but you should also make sense of them. Don't rely on facts, figures and quotes to tell the story for you: *interpret* them for the reader.

For example, in Louis Nowra's play *Così* the social worker Justin says of the mental institution inmates: 'They're just normal people' but then contradicts himself, saying: 'They are normal people who have done extraordinary things, thought extraordinary thoughts'.

But so what? We can develop the point further:

> The social worker, who is in a professional care role, shows confusion about the division between 'normal' and mad. If even the professionals have a confused perspective on the differences between sanity and madness, what hope does the outsider Lewis have of perceiving the difference and communicating with the inmates effectively?

One detail has now been developed to make a more significant statement. Statistics usually need further discussion to explain their true significance: it is not enough to quote the current Balance of Payments figures, or the latest unemployment numbers; we need to know whether they are better or worse than expected, what effects they may have on other aspects of the economy, and so on.

Advanced skills 1: *analysis*

One difference between an average essay and a very good one can be that the better responses demonstrate a *critical* understanding of the issue. In other words, you don't take ideas for granted, but probe them further. Careful analysis of the following examples reveals that there are problems with the logic.

1 'Software piracy has always existed, so it always will.' This is a lazy argument that has no logical proof or reasoning. This kind of piracy was not a problem in Ancient Greece!

2 'Any true Australian will believe in the flag we now fly as the one true flag.' There are a couple of problems with this idea: first of all, what is a 'true Australian'? Are Aboriginal peoples, Torres Strait Islanders and migrants 'true Australians'?' The speaker doesn't clarify the point but seems to be making a vague, emotional appeal.

3 'Arnold is an idiot, so anything he says can't be relied upon.' Arnold is truly in a bad way if this statement is literally true! Arguments should be based on logic, not personal attack.

4 'World weather patterns are definitely changing. I've never seen a November like this.' World weather patterns are indeed changing, but the speaker certainly can't deduce this from their limited life experience, nor speak of the 'world' from one part of the globe only.

5 'World War I was inevitable. Therefore so were all of the following events.' There are two assertions which are challengeable here: firstly that the war was inevitable and secondly that its outbreak directly caused all succeeding events.

6 'I don't know what you're talking about; it's a load of rubbish.' Just because they don't understand it, doesn't mean it's wrong!

7 'Business is designed to meet public needs, so what's good for business is good for everybody.' Not necessarily, and not always! There is no real logical connection here.

8 'Because computers were designed by scientists, they have always been handy tools for scientists.' Many other things designed by scientists aren't of much use to them!

Learn to check the logic of your statements carefully, to test them out for yourself. Do they really 'hold water'?

Advanced skills 1: *fluency*

In English, you are marked (in part) on your ability to express yourself fluently and clearly in writing. This comes with practice of course, with wider reading and greater familiarity with language. But you should learn to look at your early drafts critically and find ways to improve them. This example is from the introduction of a student's first draft social study essay.

> To answer most accurately what a total institution is, I *have quoted* Erving Goffman. I *have then* outlined the four *aspects believed essential to encompass being titled a* total institution, (she then lists these four points) ... (italics are mine)

While the wording is still awkward at this stage, the general point can be understood: the writer is using Goffman's definition of a 'total institution', and will use four aspects of this definition. However, it is rather odd to say 'I have quoted' at the beginning of an essay, especially when she hasn't quoted him yet. To *quote* means to reproduce that writer's words exactly. What she means is that she is *referring* to Goffman's approach.

It is not usual to use the past tense in this way, as she does with 'I have quoted' and 'I have then outlined', especially at the start of an essay. We might use it later on, or in the conclusion: 'As I have shown ...' Generally one writes an English essay in the present tense. (See the sample essay in Chapter 6.) At times you can use the future tense here, as I have done with the italicised words in the revised passage on the following page.

'Aspects believed essential to encompass being titled' is a rather hefty barrage of words, but what does it mean? For a start, *who* 'believes' this, and what does she mean by 'encompass being titled'? Impressive as the word 'encompass' is, it's not used quite accurately here. When in doubt it's easier to use plain words. Here's how a better version might look:

> To explain what a total institution is, reference *will be made* to Erving Goffman, and in particular to his description of the four characteristics of a total institution: ...

Let's consider some of the changes made:

- Replacing 'answer' with 'explain'—the first word is not completely 'wrong', but the second belongs to the formal *register* (level) of essay English and is more suitable
- Leaving out 'most accurately'—this phrase is not particularly helpful. On whose authority is this 'most accurate'? ('When in doubt, leave it out'.)
- Simplifying 'aspects believed essential to encompass being titled'—this pile-up of words gives the impression of uncertainty, hidden behind a wall of vague verbiage
- Using a colon at the end of this sentence instead of a comma—why? A colon is often used to introduce a list or some major point. Commas are used to separate words in a list, or different parts of the sentence from each other.

We can learn a number of things from this one example: that using fewer words can actually say 'more'. Get straight to the point, don't hide behind vague phrases and long strings of words, and don't use 'fancy words' unless you are sure of their meaning. (Once I explained the meaning of the word 'vocation'—a 'calling'—and asked a student to use it in a sentence. He came up with: 'My mother vocationed me in to dinner'. No, that's not quite right!)

These are key skills for improving your expression: clarifying your meaning; and correcting grammar, word choice and punctuation. Linda Flower, in her book *Problem Solving Strategies for Writing*, comments that early drafts tend to be 'writer based'—they help the writer to get their ideas out, and tend to be structured according to the order in which thoughts came to the writer. That is a good start, but the good essay needs to transform that writer-based first draft into a reader-based, 'user friendly' essay with improved expression and structure.

A training run: *the five-paragraph essay*

In this chapter, we have looked at some of the microskills that contribute to a good essay. Now it's time to practise writing on the *macro* scale, putting it all together.

The five-paragraph essay is a very simple (but limited!) short essay form that gives good practice with the basics of essay structure. Simple as it is, few people 'get it right' first off. They have difficulty conforming to the rigid rules, and can't resist the urge to break them in some way!

Think of this form as a kind of game, or as a special challenge. The rules are simple: the five-paragraph essay allows you to advance an argument in the first paragraph, discuss three points to support it (one paragraph each), and cap it off in the final paragraph.

How to write a five-paragraph essay in eight steps

1. Choose any topic with which you are very familiar: any subject, topic or English text you have already studied. Ask yourself a question about it, e.g., 'What is the writer trying to say?' or 'What do we know about the ancient Etruscans?'.
2. On a blank sheet of paper, write a brief answer in no more than a sentence. For example, 'The Australian poet Bruce Dawe is criticising the inanity of some aspects of modern life.'

3 Underneath this, list three points that support your argument.

Dawe criticises:

- the mass media
- consumerism
- lack of depth in conversation.

4 Draft your *first paragraph*. This paragraph must:

a state your argument

b list the three points that support it.

(*Do not fail to do this!* This makes you plan ahead, from the very start.) If you have a clear idea of how to cap this argument off, then you could also refer to the final conclusion in some way, e.g. 'It will be seen that ... '

5 *Second paragraph*: Discuss your main, first point in full, giving details and relating it to your argument.

6 *Third paragraph:* Do the same, for the second point.

7 *Fourth paragraph:* Do the same, as for the third point.

8 *Conclusion:* Summarise the previous discussion and try to cap it off somehow.

If you stick closely to the rules of the five-paragraph essay, you will see that it isn't really a hard trick; you'll soon decide it's rather boring and limiting. That also means that the essay form is actually really easy! But make sure you do produce at least one such essay, conforming completely to the rules. Use the method described above as your checklist and ask a friend to check it for you.

Congratulations! You've mastered the basic essay structure!

EXERCISES

1 Read the following sample essay and underline all topic sentences.

2 Underline the sentence that states the essay's main argument.

3 Find as many 'linking' words as you can.

4 What other microskills does this essay use?

5 Check this essay against the five-paragraph essay method described above. Does it meet all the requirements?

Sample five-paragraph essay: Learning to write

One of the most confounding problems for the novice essay writer is the notion that writing is a talent that you either 'have' or don't have. The reality is quite different, however: this 'talent' is acquired by practice, by the development of separate microskills, and by getting guidance and feedback from a sensitive reader. It will be shown that work in these three areas will produce real progress, in time.

Many people who come back to study after years of absence complain that their mind has gone 'rusty', or that they find it hard to 'get into gear'. This suggests that writing and study are like physical activity: practising frequent, short periods of writing at regular intervals develops your mental 'fitness' better than a weekly study 'workout' after which you forget everything for another week. The essay writer needs regular practice, specifically with essays, and one more ingredient: a little time ... No-one gets 'fit' overnight.

The macroskill of writing is actually a combination of many different microskills — smaller skills needed in the writing process. Some of the more important of these are: sustaining an argument, organising data, expressing ideas clearly and concisely, and 'signposting'. Learning to write can be approached by working on these skills separately, or in various combinations, before they are all brought together in the essay itself.

If writing is, as the saying goes, 'a lonely business', the process of learning how to write doesn't really need to be. In fact, it is preferable to find someone to act as your 'mentor' or guide, reading your early drafts and helping you improve them. Your mentor can be a parent, older brother or sister, family friend, or anyone who understands writing. However, good mentors can be hard to find: make sure that yours is not only knowledgeable, but that they give you *positive* feedback and reassurance, and can show you how to improve on weaknesses. If you can afford it, a professional tutor is often the best help you will get in 'unlocking' your potential.

It has been demonstrated that the 'talent' of essay writing is, in fact, a skill, and that it can be learnt. Some key inputs to your learning process should be regular practice, the development of specific skills, and expert guidance. Once this skill is developed, your new-found 'talent' can be your key to the universe, for writing skills can help you get into your desired university or TAFE course and, beyond that, into the job of your dreams. In fact, if you continue to keep your mind 'fit', you'll use these skills throughout your career!

5 Preparing for essays

In all subjects, as I said before, your essay can only be as good as the amount of study you've put into it. So before we look at putting the various skills together (see Chapter 6), it's important to discuss studying for essays.

And by the way, now that you are aware of 'linking', you should recognise that I am 'welding' this chapter with the previous and the following chapters, by referring to the link between the skills discussed in Chapter 4, and how they will be used in Chapter 6.

Studying for essays involves:

- time organisation
- focused study
- note-taking
- reading strategies.

It is possible to write an essay without having much to say. 'Waffle' tends to be full of vague terms, generalisations and half-thought-out ideas ... 'you know?' The writer might imagine that it 'looks alright' but in fact such essays are quickly spotted by experienced readers. One of the big shocks of the HSC years for many students is that the last-minute, studyless, just-dreamt-up-the-night-before essay doesn't do so well anymore. You will find this even more so at university or TAFE.

If you haven't researched, read widely, taken notes and thought carefully about your topic, you're not ready to write a good essay. You should, if possible, work out a rough essay plan before even starting to research an essay, to help you focus on the kind of information you need.

Let's look at these four key study skills:

Time organisation

To write a good essay takes time, so make time to give yourself the best chance.

- Start straightaway. Yes: the very day you're given the essay question, look at it carefully and ask yourself a few questions:
- What information would be required to answer the question?
- Do I know enough about the topic?
- What extra information do I need?
- What thoughts do I have about it at this stage?

I have said that the essay is like a par 3–4 golf hole, because it takes several shots to accomplish. Also, like golf, you get nowhere at all until you have at least teed off! Even if the first shot is woefully misdirected or dribbles to a miserable halt, you have made some progress. When you next strike, you should have a better sense of where you're headed, more determination and, hopefully, a better aim once you've warmed up. With the essay, luckily, you don't lose points with each extra stroke you make: in fact, the more work you put into it, the better your essay usually is, up to a certain point.

- 'Incubate'. Let the ideas develop in your mind. Once you have come to a point where you simply can't think further about it, stop. It's surprising what ideas can hatch out days later, even when you're not consciously thinking about the topic. But until you do the initial thinking, you won't hatch anything. Planning in advance offers this advantage of making best use of your time, even when you're not studying! You can literally 'sleep on it'.

Focused study

Some students develop very inefficient study habits. The two extremes are: to read one book and take massive notes, virtually rewriting the book word for word, or, on the other hand, to write virtually nothing, trusting in memory completely. The first method of course will give you a pile of unwieldy 'junk'; the second will give you very little at all. As we see on the following page, it is better to consult several books or other sources in less detail than to read only one, from cover to cover, including information that has no bearing on your study.

Focused study for essays means that you know what you are looking for, what is needed and what is not. Before starting your reading and research, make a list of all information you need, under separate headings. Under each heading write brief notes about what you know. Leave plenty of space under each one to add extra information, or use a separate sheet of paper for each. Also make a list of your specific questions: what 'proofs' are you looking for? What facts, figures or issues call for more information?

When re-reading an English text it is usually helpful to take notes as you go, under thematic headings such as 'Characters', 'Plot', 'Themes', etc. Likewise, you can take notes as you watch the video or DVD of a movie, pausing occasionally, or download relevant internet material directly into organised computer folders. (Always remember to note the source and paste the URL into your file for reference.)

Note-taking

There are many different ways of note-taking, none of them the sole correct form. Your notes are for you only; the most important thing is that they be easily identifiable, organised, clear, readable and sufficiently complete so that, when you come back to read them some months later, they are still understandable. Whether you use a system of folders, cards, computer files or whatever, find an organised system that works well for you.

It is very helpful to make your system flexible so that your notes can be rearranged easily for essay-writing purposes. All your notes on characters, for example, might be on single loose leaves. Single sheets can be more helpful than lumping everything together in an exercise book. Use plenty of headings and subheadings (so that you can quickly find the right information). For computer notes, save them in appropriate directories and subdirectories to make files easy to locate.

Common student errors are:

- taking notes randomly (whatever feels right)
- writing down large chunks of information for no defined purpose
- writing out whole pages word for word from the book (Are you learning anything?).

Tip:

Work out your own 'shorthand' notation: it is handy to use symbols and abbreviations for commonly used words.

Use the first letter of a key term, capitalised, with a full stop after it: in English you might use L. for 'language'.

Other suggestions:

∴	therefore
+	also, in addition
→	(this led to ...)
<	less than, smaller or came before
>	greater than, after, more important

Use standard symbols from different subjects, e.g., in Economics, 'Y' means 'income'.

Make up your own 'shorthand' for often-repeated words, as the need arises. Some symbols or abbreviations could be used for all subjects, whereas others might relate to one subject only. If there's a danger of forgetting what it stands for when you re-read later, write a 'key' to these abbreviations somewhere on the first page of your notes.

(Computer users can use macros to write commonly used words, or 'Search/Replace' options. By using the code 'e=', and later searching and replacing this 'string', I need type the word 'essay' once only for this entire book!)

Reading strategies

Reading becomes increasingly important in the HSC years, and is even more so with university and TAFE studies. Since you won't have time to read all textbooks and other sources 'cover to cover', you need to become familiar with different ways of using them. There are different ways of reading, and you should learn to vary your methods according to your purpose and to the style of the writing itself. If a book is particularly detailed and you need only general information, don't read it 'word for word'.

Reading is all about **anticipation**. Half-way through a sentence, we can often guess what's about to come next. (Do you ever finish sentences for people who are talking to you? It's a similar process.) Knowing the structure of writing also helps you read, anticipate and absorb more efficiently.

Books are usually structured 1–2–3 just like essays. They have an introduction, a body and a conclusion. You know that an introduction should give you the main argument and introduce key topics. More detail on each point will be found in the body of the essay. You can look for a final summing up, to see how the argument has progressed or what final points are made, in the conclusion.

Selective reading

Wide reading is most helpful, but you certainly don't have to read every text available on a subject. Nor do you need to read every section and every page of every book you consult. Different works have different strengths, so look at a range of them first before deciding which ones seem to offer you most. Concentrate on the Contents and Index, looking for your focus topics. Read the Introduction quickly, and some of the first chapter, to get a general idea of the book. Sample a page at random to see if the writing is suited to your purposes. (Is it too technical or jargonistic? Is the writer focused on themes that are unhelpful to you?)

Once you have chosen your reading sources, be selective in how you read them too, since not all sections may be helpful. A book is much easier to read the second time around, because you now have the 'big picture', and you know how sections relate to the whole work. So a preliminary skim or speed-read can make a full reading far more fruitful, as you'll absorb more information.

In your first reading, try not to use a dictionary very much. Often an unfamiliar word's meaning will become clear, especially if it's used often. You don't need to know the dictionary meaning of every word, so long as you can follow the discussion comfortably. Stopping too often slows you down and can lead to losing the thread of the argument. During a detailed reading, look up unfamiliar words, especially if they are used often. A good vocabulary is a great asset, now and for later study, and the best way to build one up is slowly, over time; so start now!

NOTE: Here again, English is different to other essay-writing subjects because you do need to focus closely on the use of language. You should certainly read or view your prescribed texts fully and thoroughly, and at least twice. On your second, more detailed reading, look up unfamiliar words in a dictionary. You can practise selective reading when looking for supplementary material.

Skimming

Skimming is reading sections only, skipping to find the next section of interest. Concentrate on following the main ideas and blocking out detail. To read a chapter, it's a good idea to read the introductory paragraphs in full, then focus on topic sentences.

Scanning

In scanning you look only for a particular word or set of words, ignoring all else, and glancing over the pages rapidly. This has less value as a study skill, but it can help you find a particular passage quickly, or any references to one particular word or concept.

'Speed-reading'

It is possible to undertake short courses in this helpful skill. Don't get carried away by exaggerated claims, but it's certainly possible to build up a powerful Effective Reading Rate. (This term is a measure of how quickly one reads, compared to how much one absorbs and understands.) If you have time and money, and expect to do tertiary studies involving a lot of reading, this could be a good investment. Some selective colleges in the United States are said to require a minimum reading speed of 500 words per minute!

The key approach of speed-reading is not to read texts word for word but to 'open your eyes', your field of vision, and take in larger chunks of words at a time. It is a good start to practise concentrating on phrases, instead of single words.

6 Essay writing 'by numbers'

Assuming that you have thoroughly researched your essay and organised your notes, you are ready to start the first draft. I jokingly call this chapter 'essay writing by numbers' but of course writing is never as automatic as just joining the dots: it involves making choices in knowledge, argument, organisation and word usage. Unlike painting by numbers, the art of essay writing is a genuinely creative one.

The method described here is only a suggested approach to help get you started; the more familiar you become with essays, the more you'll be able to find your own methods. Be prepared to experiment.

The method is summarised in the following pages and each point is then discussed in detail, just as the five-paragraph essay announces your points in advance and then expands on them. (However, in most essay writing, you cannot use point form.)

Before we look at this method, read the following sample essay. This essay is then reprinted with various comments and explanations. For those who are not familiar with the prescribed text, a short summary is given first. This is NOT part of the essay itself!

Summary of selected poems of Kenneth Slessor

Kenneth Slessor was a Sydney-based poet and journalist who wrote most of his poetry in the first half of the 20th century. Slessor turned away from the Australian bush ballad tradition to write on urban themes. His work shows an interest in experimentation, an interest that he shared with Literary Modernist writers of his time. Literary Modernism was a movement characterised by often-radical experiments in literary form, especially in poetry and prose.

The selection of Slessor poems is diverse, ranging from poetic meditations upon time ('Out of Time' and 'Wild Grapes'), to social observation of the once-bohemian Kings Cross, near where he lived ('William Street'), through to a response to a scene from Jonathan Swift's satirical novel *Gulliver's Travels* ('Gulliver'), based on a scene where Gulliver finds himself in the land of the little people, pegged to the ground by his arms, legs and hair. He also addresses historical themes, from Australia's colonial convict past ('Vesper-Song of the Reverend Samuel Marsden') to World War II ('Beach Burial'), in which he saw service as a war correspondent.

The secondary text selected (Humphries, 2018) is a short satirical piece broadcast on ABC television as a segment within the current affairs show *7.30*, in which Mark Humphries offered a witty satirical response to events in November 2018: a series of strikes and demonstrations held by Australian school students to protest the lack of government action to prevent the potentially catastrophic results of climate change.

The following sample essay is not perfect and there are many other ways in which the question could have been answered. You may well disagree with the argument and with various points made; the purpose, however, is to illustrate the structure of an essay and some of the techniques involved in writing one. Look up any terms that are unclear to you.

Sample essay: Common module in English—Texts and Human Experiences

Show how study of your prescribed text, and at least one other text, has deepened your understanding of how texts represent human experiences.

1 The selected poems of Kenneth Slessor represent human experiences, both individual and collective, as being affected by two primary forces: Time, personified, and the influence of people who exert their power or authority. In relation to Time, Slessor suggests in 'Out of Time' two contrasting experiences: 'Time, the wave', which buffets us but then passes over, and 'Time, the bony knife' that penetrates immediately, leaving a lasting effect—both being primarily destructive in their effects. This theme is reflected in other poems by Slessor, such as 'Wild Grapes' and 'Beach Burial'. The experience of destructiveness is also a dominant theme in his portrayal of the influence of others, which is portrayed as punitive ('Vesper-Song of the Reverend Samuel Marsden') or otherwise hurtful ('Beach Burial' and 'Gulliver'). However, there are also hints in his poetry of a different experience of Time; one that allows us to step briefly 'out of Time', to turn one's attention away from these forces and to attend instead to our interior self in a dialogue with one's 'own heart'. This alternative form of experience is explored further in a selected text based on a topical event: strikes by Australian school students in November 2018. It is demonstrated that even though the possibilities of this interior-based experience are more substantial than Slessor suggests, individuals pursuing this mode are likely to find it hard to extricate themselves, both from forces of Time and from the influence of others, including authority.

2 One of Slessor's most powerful poems, 'Out of Time', represents Time as an inescapable and ultimately destructive force, in terms of its effects on individual experience. Of the two forms of Time which he identifies, 'Time, the wave' is portrayed in figurative language that represents it as a force of nature, as in the imagery where Time, like the wind, 'fills the sails of a hundred yachts'. In other images he represents Time as 'flowing', like a river, or flying like a bird 'behind the daylight'. 'Time, the wave' at first appears innocuous and purely transitory. The text draws an analogy between Time and a wave: it simply bends us like seaweed and

passes us by. This lulls the reader into an initial impression that 'Time, the wave' is benign as it is first represented as 'enfolding' the first-person narrator in their bed, a cosy and comforting image that one associates with feelings of being warm and safe and of being lulled to sleep. This gently evocative image contrasts strongly to 'Time, the bony knife that runs me through', a metaphor that implies the effect of a deep wound to the living body, of cutting to the bone.

3 By the end of the poem, however, this gentle experience of Time proves to be a fantasy or illusion, as in the third stanza where 'Time, the wave', now transformed into 'the suck of the sea', drowns the narrator. That 'Time, the wave' is ultimately destructive is also the implicit theme in 'Wild Grapes', which is an extended meditation on time past in a now-ruined orchard, a place that has sustained a series of losses, like the cherries and apples. Slessor conveys this sense of loss by pointing to the beauty of what has been lost in the striking simile of 'apples bright as dogstars'. Again Time is represented as a force of nature, one that takes over as soon as humans fail to keep up the orchard actively. Its effects are not confined to nature but also impact on human experience, as seen when Slessor singles out the 'vanished Mulligans' and 'Hartigans, long drowned in earth themselves'. The imagery in this phrasing is in close agreement with the Time that drowns like the suck of the sea in 'Out of Time', but the paradoxical expression 'drowned in earth' conveys his sense that it is Time, not literal waves, that brings oblivion. Similarly the 'convoy' of dead sailors floating in the sea in 'Beach Burial' is another expression of Time's destructive flow. This expression too is a paradox: a convoy is a purposeful movement of a group of boats, whereas the ghostly convoy of corpses has no apparent purpose, no taking of sides between warring forces. Through this use of paradox Slessor undercuts the images of Time as purely a force of nature in showing that it is strongly affected by human action: the orchard fails when humans fail to maintain it, while the dead sailors are victims of human action, not an abstract force of Time.

4 Undercutting the somewhat overwhelming, unstoppable force of 'Time, the wave', Slessor draws our attention to the importance of how we engage with Time. He suggests that this goes beyond how we respond practically to Time's force in everyday experiences, to how we engage it in words and thoughts. For example, in 'Wild Grapes' the narrative voice responds imaginatively to the name and appearance of the wild Isabella grapes, producing the image of a girl called Isabella: 'A girl half-fierce, half-melting, as these grapes'. It is in the narrator's imagination that the

girl 'has lingered on defiantly' when Time has obliterated any concrete trace of her. Likewise, the primary emphasis in 'Beach Burial' is on the simple inscription '*Unknown seaman*', in which the 'purple drips' of the 'ghostly pencil' are compared to the blue of 'drowned men's lips'. This emphasis is conveyed in part by Slessor's single use of rhyme in this poem; that is, 'drips'/'lips'.

5 Therefore in both poems it is implied that it is important to make meaning of human experience because the meaning we make is what may endure in the wake of Time's 'golden undertow'. This beautiful image, evoking the dying light of the sinking sun, conveys that Time brings both the experience of a life full of sunshine and optimism, and decline. What is left in Time's wake, in spoken language or inscriptions, is an enduring image of human experience. This also applies to the work of the poet.

6 Most of 'Out of Time' is focused on 'Time, the wave', represented figuratively as a gentle force of nature. Slessor's 'Time, the bony knife', on the other hand, implies an aggressive force wielded by others as it 'drills me, drives through bone and vein': only humans use knives. Through these forceful verbs he conveys in imagery that Time can be wielded like a weapon that wounds instantaneously. A similarly penetrative and wounding effect is figured in 'Vesper-Song of the Reverend Samuel Marsden', which focuses on the punitive exercise of power or authority by the 'flogging parson', the Reverend Samuel Marsden. Although his authority is supposedly spiritual rather than penal power, Marsden is represented as being primarily interested in administering the lash to those whom he considers to have sinned, more than in his supposed spiritual calling. His interest in secular power, more than spiritual authority, is expressed in his legalistic language: his victims are 'twice convicted'—of moral failings in addition to past crimes. Slessor's Marsden is more interested in punishing convicts further than in improving them through the teaching and practice of his own religious 'convictions'. His un-Christian attitude of contempt for sinners is conveyed in the image of a 'cage of brutes' whom he invites to 'lick and learn at these my boots'. Indeed, he is represented as revelling in this display of his own power.

7 The related pun on soul/sole in which he metaphorically treats the eternal human soul as little more than a worn shoe 'sole' implies that he is more interested, rather sadistically, in the 'stripes of jewelled blood' he inflicts on mortal human flesh than in leading sinners to repentance and enlightenment. Rather, he seeks to (en)grave 'another Testament' on the

convicts' naked flesh. The language used to convey this is deceptive, however, as Marsden claims to want to heal their souls through this different kind of 'Testament'. A similar approach is seen in the pun on the word 'welt', which in context refers to a repair made using a leather strap. However, a welt is also a scar, a witness of Time's impact. Thus, although Marsden is represented as wanting to be seen as doing good deeds for God—'Not mine, the glory that endures, / but Yours, dear God, entirely Yours'—in reality he is sadistically interested in displaying his power and importance, and in inflicting pain.

8 In summary, Slessor's representation of human experience—between 'Time, the wave' and 'Time, the knife'—appears bleak. Time brings sunshine and night, good times and bad, but ultimately it destroys us. In fact time itself can be a punishment: Gulliver would prefer to be hanged, to end his time, rather than to endure the punishing experience where he has been pinned to the ground and tries to extract himself hair by hair. In 'Gulliver' Slessor draws an extended analogy between Gulliver's experience of the 'tyranny of sinews' and the many various things we may experience in life: 'love, hunger ... age'. The poem suggests that human experiences in various forms can resemble a prison, 'doing time' like Marsden's convicts, but without literal walls or chains. Thus experience itself is a 'net' from which it is hard to escape, just as it seems impossible to escape from Time itself. In 'Out of Time' the pattern of echoing the last line of the previous stanza at the head of the following stanza reinforces this sense of experience as an inescapable net.

9 Slessor does, however, also hint in 'Out of Time' at the possibility of respite from Time, and from experience, by listening to one's own heart: an instrument that also beats Time, but to its own rhythm. By retreating within, one can seize a 'lovely moment' while 'Time, the wave', in contrast, must hurry on to keep its appointments. The individual experience of this moment, of becoming 'fleshless and ageless, changeless and made free', is represented in the beautiful image of a glittering sunlit world captured in a photographic image in a bubble.

10 Nonetheless, this escape from the hubbub, from the flowing currents of everyday life, is perhaps only an illusion. The individual capacity for introspection is represented by Slessor as only momentary, and illusory. The phrase 'out of Time' signifies a moment of freedom, of escaping Time, but the expression also has a double meaning in implying that it comes too late for the subject of the poem, who has now run 'out of Time'. Slessor also conveys in imagery that this third kind of experience of Time is perhaps just an insubstantial 'bubble', as the connotations of that word

suggest. Ultimately there appears to be little sense in Slessor's poetry of a viable alternative to the unstoppable force of Time.

11 Thus Slessor's third option of introspection, of stepping 'out of Time' to consult one's own heart, is not represented as a substantial alternative to Time, in nature or in society. However, a satirical television sketch (Humphries, 2018) examines a topical story where individuals, acting collectively, attempt a very different approach to Time. This short piece responds to a series of events in which students mounted collective action in the form of school strikes. Not content to rest, trapped like 'Gulliver' in the net of inadequate responses to climate change, these students attempted to take an active role in determining not merely their own future but that of the planet. It will be demonstrated that in response to these actions, Humphries satirically represents the Federal Government as responding in two primary and somewhat contradictory ways: firstly by attempting to win students over by persuasive means and secondly through the use of threats.

12 From the opening frames of the television sketch the government is represented as attempting to appeal to school students: Humphries's character in a close-up shot tries to demonstrate empathy by brightly asking 'How are you enjoying puberty?'. This clumsy opening gambit is followed by a scene in which he is riding in a dodgem car, apparently to emphasise what a fun person this 'spokesdude for Youths [sic] Affairs' is. This absurd coining is accompanied by the use of an informal language register ('g'day') and slang ('youse kids'), presumably to reinforce this effect. In addition he uses phrases such as 'totally lit' and 'throwing shade' in an attempt to create the impression of a government that is 'keeping up' with the times.

13 The approach that the government is represented as pursuing is to persuade by personal appeal more than with logic or argument. It tempts youths to identify with this person who, by acting young and 'hip', tries to be seen as someone just like them, who might share similar aims and interests. Another way this is pursued is through direct appeal, as the Humphries character, acting as if he is a friend, pretends to takes us into his confidence: 'I'll level with you, kids, this whole situation has made our prime minister very upset—not climate change. I'm talking about your little protest'.

14 However, the language betrays a similar technique to 'Vesper-Song of the Reverend Samuel Marsden' in pursuing a double agenda: of wanting to be seen in one light while in reality pursuing a different agenda to the

supposed one. It is the contradictory nature of Humphries's language that betrays his true intent. In dismissing the idea of the prime minister not being upset about climate change he thus raises the suggestion that he should be. Likewise, there is a subtle connotation of dismissal in his use of the adjective 'little', as if to imply that the thoughts and actions of these 'kids' are really of no account in the adult world of politics; that is, that they should accept their relative lack of power and the government's lack of effective and lasting action on climate change: 'I think it would be totally lit for you to maintain the status quo and stay in class'. This suggests that behind the persuasive appeal, the encouragement to identify with the spokesdude, and thus with the government, is a coercive agenda. The occasional slips into more formal language, such as 'maintain the status quo', also unmask his true agenda of supporting the government's stance on climate change.

15 This strategy of an attempted appeal to students is taken further in a later scene, where the spokesdude, dressed as a student, attempts to incite other students to protest against a Labor proposal to drop tax advantages for shareholders. This demonstrates two things: firstly that the spokesman is truly not one of the school students and secondly that the government would be happy for students to protest about an issue on which they themselves were in agreement. They are not speaking from firmly held principles (students should attend school and keep away from politics) but are simply seeking political advantage: in other words, they are clearly hypocritical.

16 This impression of politics over principle is reinforced by a second dominant theme in Humphries's satirical sketch: the use of attacking or threatening language. Humphries chooses to have the government represented directly, in its own words, in recent footage of parliament:

> SCOTT MORRISON, PRIME MINISTER: We do not support our schools being turned into parliaments.

This strategy cleverly exposes Morrison's own words by putting them into a broader political context, with the point of view then turning back from Morrison to Humphries's commentary, which refers to another political controversy of that time:

> COALITION SPOKESDUDE FOR YOUTH AFFAIRS: Indeed, because if schools were like our parliament, you would actually sit in class for only 13 days until April, which is a disgrace—if you did it.

Humphries stresses the word 'disgrace' and pauses after it, as if the sentence is complete and he has expressed an absolute truth. The remaining four words are added as an afterthought, with stress placed on the word 'you' in order to expose the hypocrisy of the double standard: that it is acceptable for parliament to spend very little time sitting but not for school children to take a moment 'out of Time', as in Slessor's poem, to listen to their own hearts and minds.

17 As in 'Vesper-Song of the Reverend Samuel Marsden', how we use our time and freedom is subject to hostile reactions from authorities, with the use of punishing or threatening words. Responding to the strike, where students took time out from school, the Federal Resources Minister Matt Canavan claimed that:

> The best thing you'll learn about going to a protest is how to join the dole queue. Because that's what your future life will look like, up in a line asking for a handout, not actually taking charge for your life and getting a real job. (*The Sydney Morning Herald*, 2018)

The minister's statement expresses a viewpoint apparently without any factual or logical substantiation, as there is no logical link between political protest and the very separate matter of asking for handouts in the future. In fact what students were asking for was not a handout but a future that is viable for everyone. Canavan's words appear to be an attempt to put students down. Humphries dramatises this hostile reaction discreetly: while posing as the students' 'friend', he comes across more like a government agent sending a warning:

> So don't make our prime minister angry or he'll sentence you
> to a detention so bad even the UN is like (bleep) me.

Humphries's clever pun associates the government's detention of refugees, which has been criticised by the UN, with detention in school as a kind of punishment, where time is again wielded as a weapon by authority. His use of a censored expletive both continues the attempt to appear as an everyday person, as 'one of us', while emphasising the severity of the threat. In fact the true aim appears to be more to scare the audience into submission than to offer fair warning.

18 It has been shown that when people try to follow Slessor's third path, of listening to their hearts and acting individually or collectively to shape the future through influencing policy, this can be interpreted as a challenge or even a threat by others, even when such action is sincere

and based on well-researched facts; in this instance, the very serious conclusions drawn by climate scientists. Humphries uses irony to claim that the government takes the issue 'deadly seriously': this is not consistent with the following scene, in which government members are represented directly, in footage taken at a Pacific Islands leaders' meeting on climate change in 2015. Three Australian ministers, waiting for proceedings to begin, were caught on camera and on microphone in what they believed to be a private conversation:

> PETER DUTTON: Time doesn't mean anything when you're about to have water lapping at your door.

Again, Humphries uses direct representation to damn the government in its own words: PM Tony Abbott laughs at Dutton's joke while Morrison represses a smile and looks up at the mic hanging over them. The implication that can be drawn is that they do not take climate science seriously. In Dutton's joke, the government is represented as literally laughing at the fatalistic 'Time, the wave', and as discounting the needs of the Pacific Island nations, which are greatly endangered by climate change and which, like students, have a strong stake in the future. For these students at least, time does mean something. Further, they appreciate, as implied in the unkempt orchard of 'Wild Grapes', that in some cases time only overtakes us if we allow it to.

19 The concluding line by Humphries offers another perspective on the government's attitude:

> There is never an excuse for skipping class unless it's a science class in which case we can write you a letter or something.

Again Humphries implies hypocrisy on the government's part: that despite their supposed commitment to the education of Australian youth, they will turn their minds against science if it contradicts their political agenda. The damning implication is that they would even be happy for school students not to be properly educated.

20 My understanding of human experiences has been deepened by my study of the prescribed text, which shows that Time and power are very strong influences on experiences. However, unlike its representation in 'Out of Time', Time need not be a negative experience. Rather, even though everything passes on eventually, we should seek to make the best use of the time we have, to engage actively, to extract meaning from it and from the experiences that come with it. In 'Gulliver', of the everyday aspects of life that Slessor presents as 'ridiculous manacles', some are

negative (hunger and neuralgia) but many could be seen as neutral (hot and cold) or positive (love and sleep). In addition, we have seen that it is also important that writers leave some trace behind of human experiences, just as Slessor did with his experience of being a war correspondent and his life in the colourful environs of Kings Cross.

21 It has also been shown that influence is often wielded like a weapon by those who have power or authority. Often this takes place through language, which can be used to try to appeal to people, to deceive them or even to 'lash' them, as in Marsden's whip. Again this does not mean we must expect our experience of society to always be negative. Rather, the texts considered suggest the conclusion that dialogue and dispute are an integral part of human experience. In order for us to engage in such dialogue, Slessor's third mode, of stepping 'out of Time' to listen to the heart and mind, can be the essential step required in promoting a significant wave for change, rather than accepting the passive experience of Time in 'Out of Time', where Time simply passes over us and we bend to it in response. Indeed, not to do so is to risk a more destructive future that would emerge directly out of the inadequacy of humanity's efforts to address global warming, instead of embracing the creative and positive change that can begin to take shape in the human heart and mind.

References

Note: Most of the following references are not cited in the essay, although I consulted all of them. Generally you should only list those works one is actually citing (referencing) in the essay itself. They are included here to show how a references list might look and to note some sources that you may, like myself, enjoy. *The Conversation* is a good source of information on various subjects as it features pieces written by academics for the general public.

Duffy, S 2018, 'How our minds construct the past, present and future depends on our relationship with time', 3 January, *The Conversation.*

Gaby, A and Yunkaporta, T 2018, 'Explainer: the seasonal 'calendars' of Indigenous Australia', 3 January, *The Conversation.*

Humphries, M 2018, Satirist Mark Humphries looks at the planned school students' strike for climate change action, 29 November, *7.30,* presenter Leigh Sales, Australian Broadcasting Commission.

Indyk, I 2015, 'Kenneth Slessor and Time', *Sydney Review of Books.*

Kirkpatrick, P 2015, 'Reading Australia: "One Hundred Poems: 1919–1939" by Kenneth Slessor', 10 June, *Australian Book Review.*

Smith, GK 1978, 'Kenneth Slessor', *Westerly*, 23(2), pp. 51–59.

The Sydney Morning Herald, 30 November 2018, 'Climate change protest will lead to dole queue, minister tells students', retrieved from www.smh.com.au/politics/federal/climate-change-protest-will-lead-to-dole-queue-minister-tells-students-20181130-p50jbt.html.

'Dissected' version of the sample essay

The same essay is reproduced below but with comments and explanations following each paragraph.

- Paragraphs are numbered (for reference only—do not number paragraphs in your essay!)
- The key parts of topic sentences are underlined.
- The argument statement, announcing the theme of my argument, is double underlined.
- Comments following each paragraph are in *italics.*
- Keywords from the question are in **bold type**.
- Those aspect keywords that reflect the themes I have chosen to discuss in relation to the question are in reverse type.
- I have inserted indicative headings that give a visual cue as to the outline plan of the essay. Again you should not use headings in your essay; they are purely for reference. However, you could consider using them in the drafting stages of your essay as a means of keeping track of where your argument is headed.

Introduction

1 The selected poems of Kenneth Slessor **represent human experiences**, both individual and collective, as being affected by two primary forces: Time, personified, and the influence of people who exert their power or authority. In relation to Time, Slessor suggests in 'Out of Time' two contrasting experiences—'Time, the wave', which buffets us but then passes over, and 'Time, the bony knife' that penetrates immediately, leaving a lasting effect—both being primarily destructive in their effects. This theme is reflected in other poems by Slessor such as 'Wild Grapes' and 'Beach Burial'. The experience of destructiveness is also a dominant theme in his portrayal of the influence of others, which is portrayed as

punitive ('Vesper-Song of the Reverend Samuel Marsden'), or otherwise hurtful ('Beach Burial' and 'Gulliver'). However, there are also hints in his poetry of a different experience of Time; one that allows us to step briefly 'out of Time', to turn one's attention away from these forces and to attend instead to our interior self, in a dialogue with one's 'own heart'. This alternative form of experience is explored further in a selected text based on a topical event: strikes launched by Australian school students in November 2018. It is demonstrated that, even though the possibilities of this interior-based experience are more substantial than Slessor suggests, individuals pursuing this mode are likely to find it hard to extricate themself, both from forces of Time and from the influence of others, including authority.

This first paragraph accomplishes three important things. Firstly by 'echoing' the question it puts the essay on track. Secondly it introduces some aspects I choose to examine (reverse type), and thirdly, it states my own thesis (double-underlined).

Notice that this argument takes a somewhat different viewpoint to Slessor. It is perfectly acceptable to do so; we need not assume any author is unquestionably right, nor that perspectives from long ago are still applicable today. Similarly we need not assume that one critic offers the only worthwhile viewpoint on any given text.

The last line extends the thesis, stated in the first sentence, into a 'so-what' statement anticipating the conclusion. This is not essential in an introduction.

Section 1: 'Time, the wave'

1.1 'Time, the wave' as a gentle experience

2 One of Slessor's most powerful poems, 'Out of Time' **represents** Time as an inescapable and ultimately destructive force, in terms of its effects on individual **experience**. Of the two forms of Time which he identifies, 'Time, the wave' is portrayed in figurative language that represents it as a force of nature, as in the imagery where Time, like the wind, 'fills the sails of a hundred yachts'. In other images he represents Time as 'flowing', like a river, or flying like a bird 'behind the daylight'. 'Time, the wave' at first appears innocuous and purely transitory. The text draws an analogy between Time and a wave: it simply bends us like seaweed and passes us by. This lulls the reader into an initial impression that 'Time, the wave' is benign as it is first represented as 'enfolding' the first-person narrator in their bed, a cosy and comforting image that one associates

with feelings of being warm and safe and of being lulled to sleep. This gently evocative image contrasts strongly to 'Time, the bony knife that runs me through', a metaphor that implies the effect of a deep wound to the living body, of cutting to the bone.

The introduction listed three themes to be explored: Time, the influence of others and listening to one's own heart. This first paragraph in the body of the essay introduces the first of these themes—Time, the wave—in the topic sentence, which is not on this occasion the opening sentence.

An analogy is defined in the English Standard Stage 6 Syllabus as 'A comparison demonstrating the similarities between two things, people or situations'.

1.2 'Time, the wave' as destructive

3 By the end of the poem, however, this gentle experience of Time proves to be a fantasy or illusion, as in the third stanza where 'Time, the wave', now transformed into 'the suck of the sea', drowns the narrator. That 'Time, the wave' is ultimately destructive is also the implicit theme in 'Wild Grapes', which is an extended meditation on time past in a now-ruined orchard, a place that has sustained a series of losses, like the cherries and apples. Slessor conveys this sense of loss by pointing to the beauty of what has been lost in the striking simile of 'apples bright as dogstars'. Again Time is **represented** as a force of nature, one that takes over as soon as humans fail to keep up the orchard actively. Its effects are not confined to nature but also impact on human **experience**, as seen when Slessor singles out the 'vanished Mulligans' and 'Hartigans, long drowned in earth themselves'. The imagery in this phrasing is in close agreement with the Time that drowns like the suck of the sea in 'Out of Time', but the paradoxical expression 'drowned in earth' conveys his sense that it is Time, not literal waves, that brings oblivion. Similarly the 'convoy' of dead sailors floating in the sea in 'Beach Burial' is another expression of Time's destructive flow. This expression too is a paradox: a convoy is a purposeful movement of a group of boats, whereas the ghostly convoy of corpses has no apparent purpose, no taking of sides between warring forces. Through this use of paradox Slessor undercuts the images of Time as purely a force of nature in showing that it is strongly affected by **human** action: the orchard fails when humans fail to maintain it, while the dead sailors are victims of human action, not an abstract force of Time.

The word 'however' in line 1 above is an example of signposting the argument, of indicating where the discussion is leading. For a definition of 'paradox' see the 'Some language terms' section in Chapter 8 of this book.

The term 'dogstar' is not a mere invention of Slessor's but refers to the star Sirius, which has various associations in history and mythology. With poetry in particular it is a good idea to look up the meaning of words in a dictionary as poets often employ unusual words, or common words used in uncommon senses.

4 Undercutting the somewhat overwhelming, unstoppable force of 'Time, the wave', Slessor draws our attention to the importance of how we engage with Time. He suggests that this goes beyond how we respond practically to Time's force in everyday **experiences**, to how we engage it in words and thoughts. For example, in 'Wild Grapes', the narrative voice responds imaginatively to the name and appearance of the wild Isabella grapes, producing the image of a girl called Isabella: 'A girl half-fierce, half-melting, as these grapes'. It is in the narrator's imagination that the girl 'has lingered on defiantly', when Time has obliterated any concrete trace of her. Likewise, the primary emphasis in 'Beach Burial' is on the simple inscription '*Unknown seaman*', in which the 'purple drips' of the 'ghostly pencil' are compared to the blue of 'drowned men's lips'. This emphasis is conveyed in part by Slessor's single use of rhyme in this poem; that is, 'drips'/'lips'.

This is an example of the discussion moving from broader themes to concrete discussion of details, as in the discussion of various quotes from the poems.

5 Therefore in both poems it is implied that it is important to make meaning of **human experience** because the meaning we make is what may endure in the wake of Time's 'golden undertow'. This beautiful image, evoking the dying light of the sinking sun, conveys that Time brings both the experience of a life full of sunshine and optimism, and decline. What is left in Time's wake, in spoken language or inscriptions, is an enduring image of human experience. This also applies to the work of the poet.

This paragraph makes an early response to the question by explaining what I have learnt from study of the prescribed text.

Section 2: Experience of the authority and force of others

2.1 Authority's use of power

6 Most of 'Out of Time' is focused on 'Time, the wave', **represented** figuratively as a gentle force of nature. Slessor's 'Time, the bony knife' on the other hand, implies an aggressive force wielded by others, as it 'drills me, drives through bone and vein': only humans use knives. Through these forceful verbs he conveys in imagery that Time can be wielded like a weapon that wounds instantaneously. A similarly penetrative and wounding effect is figured in 'Vesper-Song of the Reverend Samuel Marsden', which focuses on the punitive exercise of power or authority by the 'flogging parson', the Reverend Samuel Marsden. Although his authority is supposedly spiritual rather than penal power, Marsden is represented as being primarily interested in administering the lash to those whom he considers to have sinned, more than in his supposed spiritual calling. His interest in secular power, more than spiritual authority, is expressed in his legalistic language: his victims are 'twice convicted'—of moral failings in addition to past crimes. Slessor's Marsden is more interested in punishing convicts further than in improving them through the teaching and practice of his own religious 'convictions'. His un-Christian attitude of contempt for sinners is conveyed in the image of a 'cage of brutes' whom he invites to 'lick and learn at these my boots'. Indeed, he is represented as revelling in this display of his own power.

The first two sentences above bridge the connection between the preceding Section 1 and the next part of the essay.

Because poetry is so often condensed and compressed we may find that we have to research further in order to provide context. In this example this could include information about Samuel Marsden and convict history. The reference to verbs is an instance of employing some simple grammar terms to explain language use.

7 The related pun on soul/sole in which he metaphorically treats the eternal human soul as little more than a worn shoe 'sole' implies that he is more interested, rather sadistically, in the 'stripes of jewelled blood' he inflicts on mortal human flesh than in leading sinners to repentance and enlightenment. Rather, he seeks to (en)grave 'another Testament' on the convicts' naked flesh. The language used to convey this is deceptive, however, as Marsden claims to want to heal their souls through this different kind of 'Testament'. A similar approach is seen in the pun on the word 'welt', which in context refers to a repair made using a leather

strap. However, a welt is also a scar, a witness of Time's impact. Thus, although Marsden is represented as wanting to be seen as doing good deeds for God—'Not mine, the glory that endures, / but Yours, dear God, entirely Yours'—in reality he is sadistically interested in displaying his power and importance, and in inflicting pain.

Aside from historical or literary allusions it is often useful in the study of poetry to take a closer look at language than you may usually do. A quality etymological dictionary, which examines the origins of words, may give you more reliable definitions than many of the readily available online sources.

2.2 Mini-summary: Slessor's representation of human experience in relation to Time

8 In summary, Slessor's **representation** of human experience—between 'Time, the wave', and 'Time, the knife'—appears bleak. Time brings sunshine and night, good times and bad, but ultimately it destroys us. In fact time itself can be a punishment: Gulliver would prefer to be hanged, to end his time, rather than to endure the punishing experience where he has been pinned to the ground and tries to extract himself hair by hair. In 'Gulliver' Slessor draws an extended analogy between Gulliver's experience of the 'tyranny of sinews' and the many various things we may experience in life: 'love, hunger ... age'. The poem suggests that **human experiences** in various forms can resemble a prison, 'doing time' like Marsden's convicts, but without literal walls or chains. Thus experience itself is a 'net' from which it is hard to escape, just as it seems impossible to escape from Time itself. In 'Out of Time' the pattern of echoing the last line of the previous stanza at the head of the following stanza reinforces this sense of experience as an inescapable net.

The reference to the story of Gulliver in Lilliput is an example of intertexuality, which writers can use to achieve richness in a text. In the English Standard Stage 6 Syllabus, 'intertextuality' is defined as 'the associations or connections between one text and other texts'. You could research Jonathan Swift's novel Gulliver's Travels as background to understanding what led Slessor to base his poem on this story.

It is very useful to offer a mini-summary in key parts of an essay in order to signpost the developing argument and to show its connection to the following section.

Section 3: Experience 'out of time', through the heart

9 Slessor does, however, also hint in 'Out of Time' at the possibility of respite from Time, and from **experience**, by listening to one's own heart: an instrument that also beats Time, but to its own rhythm. By retreating within, one can seize a 'lovely moment' while 'Time, the wave', in contrast, must hurry on to keep its appointments. The individual experience of this moment, of becoming 'fleshless and ageless, changeless and made free', is **represented** in the beautiful image of a glittering sunlit world captured in a photographic image in a bubble.

10 Nonetheless, this escape from the hubbub, from the flowing currents of everyday life, is perhaps only an illusion. The individual capacity for introspection is **represented** by Slessor as only momentary, and illusory. The phrase 'out of Time' signifies a moment of freedom, of escaping Time, but the expression also has a double meaning in implying that it comes too late for the subject of the poem, who has now run 'out of time'. Slessor also conveys in imagery that this third kind of **experience of Time** is perhaps just an insubstantial 'bubble', as the connotations of that word suggest. Ultimately there appears to be little sense in Slessor's poetry of a viable alternative to the unstoppable force of Time.

The essay has been structured by the organisational principle of theme by theme. The third mode of experience of Time in Slessor's poetry is introduced in the correct place to lead logically to the next section (which is an extension of this theme) and to my selected text.

In the English Standard Stage 6 Syllabus, 'connotation' is defined as 'The nuances or shades of meaning attached to words, beyond that of their literal or dictionary meanings'. The literal meaning is called the denotation.

Section 4: School strike

11 Thus Slessor's third option of introspection, of stepping 'out of Time' to consult one's own heart, is not represented as a substantial alternative to Time, in nature or in society. However, a satirical television sketch (Humphries, 2018) examines a topical story where individuals, acting collectively, attempt a very different approach to Time. This short piece responds to a series of events in which students mounted collective action in the form of school strikes. Not content to rest, trapped like 'Gulliver' in the net of inadequate responses to climate change, these students attempted to take an active role in determining not merely their own future but that of the planet. It will be demonstrated that in

response to these actions, Humphries satirically **represents** the Federal Government as responding in two primary and somewhat contradictory ways: firstly by attempting to win students over by persuasive means and secondly through the use of threats.

'It will be demonstrated that' is one alternative to using the first person 'I' in an essay.

For simplicity's sake I have chosen to treat just one supplementary text of my own choice, although the syllabus calls for a 'range of short texts' to be studied in addition to the prescribed text.

4.1 Persuasive appeal

12 From the opening frames of the television sketch the government is represented as attempting to appeal to school students: Humphries's character in a close-up shot tries to demonstrate empathy by brightly asking 'How are you enjoying puberty?'. This clumsy opening gambit is followed by a scene in which he is riding in a dodgem car, apparently to emphasise what a fun person this 'spokesdude for Youths [sic] Affairs' is. This absurd coining is accompanied by the use of an informal language register ('g'day') and slang ('youse kids'), presumably to reinforce this effect. In addition he uses phrases such as 'totally lit' and 'throwing shade' in an attempt to create the impression of a government that is 'keeping up' with the times.

We use the word 'sic' to acknowledge an apparent grammatical or other error in the original source. 'Sic' is an abbreviation of a Latin phrase meaning 'thus was it written'.

13 The approach that the government is **represented** as pursuing is to persuade by personal appeal more than with logic or argument. It tempts youths to identify with this person who, by acting young and 'hip', tries to be seen as someone just like them, who might share similar aims and interests. Another way this is pursued is through direct appeal, as the Humphries character, acting as if he is a friend, pretends to takes us into his confidence: 'I'll level with you, kids, this whole situation has made our prime minister very upset—not climate change. I'm talking about your little protest'.

Another word for persuasion of this kind is 'rhetoric', which one can define as the art of persuasion. I have employed a less specialised term for simplicity's sake but could well have developed discussion of the use of rhetorical devices (see the glossary in the syllabus for more on this).

14 However, the language betrays a similar technique to 'Vesper-Song of the Reverend Samuel Marsden' in pursuing a double agenda: of wanting to be seen in one light while in reality pursuing a different agenda to the supposed one. It is the contradictory nature of Humphries's language that betrays his true intent. In dismissing the idea of the prime minister not being upset about climate change he thus raises the suggestion that he should be. Likewise, there is a subtle connotation of dismissal in his use of the adjective 'little', as if to imply that the thoughts and actions of these 'kids' are really of no account in the adult world of politics; that is, that they should accept their relative lack of power and the government's lack of effective and lasting action on climate change: 'I think it would be totally lit for you to maintain the status quo and stay in class'. This suggests that behind the persuasive appeal, the encouragement to identify with the spokesdude, and thus with the government, is a coercive agenda. The occasional slips into more formal language, such as 'maintain the status quo', also unmask his true agenda of supporting the government's stance on climate change.

15 This strategy of an attempted appeal to students is taken further in a later scene, where the spokesdude, dressed as a student, attempts to incite other students to protest against a Labor proposal to drop tax advantages for shareholders. This demonstrates two things: firstly that the spokesman is truly not one of the school students and secondly that the government would be happy for students to protest about an issue on which they themselves were in agreement. They are not speaking from firmly held principles (students should attend school and keep away from politics) but are simply seeking political advantage: in other words, they are clearly hypocritical.

The last words above are an example of 'capping off' a point to demonstrate what the preceding discussion amounts to: that is, what it really shows.

4.2 Threat

16 This impression of politics over principle is reinforced by a second dominant theme in Humphries's satirical sketch: the use of attacking or threatening language. Humphries chooses to have the government **represented** directly, in its own words, in recent footage of parliament:

> SCOTT MORRISON, PRIME MINISTER: We do not support our schools being turned into parliaments.

This strategy cleverly exposes Morrison's own words by putting them into a broader political context, with the point of view then turning back from Morrison to Humphries's commentary, which refers to another political controversy of that time:

> COALITION SPOKESDUDE FOR YOUTH AFFAIRS: Indeed, because if schools were like our parliament, you would actually sit in class for only 13 days until April, which is a disgrace—if you did it.

Humphries stresses the word 'disgrace' and pauses after it, as if the sentence is complete and he has expressed an absolute truth. The remaining four words are added as an afterthought, with stress placed on the word 'you' in order to expose the hypocrisy of the double standard: that it is acceptable for parliament to spend very little time sitting but not for school children to take a moment 'out of Time', as in Slessor's poem, to listen to their own hearts and minds.

When it comes to non-written texts there are of course all sorts of ways in which meaning is conveyed. Not all of these means are purely verbal.

17 As in 'Vesper-Song of the Reverend Samuel Marsden', how we use our time and freedom is subject to hostile reactions from authorities, with the use of punishing or threatening words. Responding to the strike, where students took time out from school, the Federal Resources Minister Matt Canavan claimed that:

> The best thing you'll learn about going to a protest is how to join the dole queue. Because that's what your future life will look like, up in a line asking for a handout, not actually taking charge for your life and getting a real job. (*The Sydney Morning Herald*, 2018)

The minister's statement expresses a viewpoint apparently without any factual or logical substantiation, as there is no logical link between political protest and the very separate matter of asking for handouts in the future. In fact what students were asking for was not a handout but a future that is viable for everyone. Canavan's words appear to be an attempt to put students down. Humphries dramatises this hostile reaction discreetly: while posing as the students' 'friend', he comes across more like a government agent sending a warning:

> So don't make our prime minister angry or he'll sentence you to a detention so bad even the UN is like (bleep) me.

Humphries's clever pun associates the government's detention of refugees, which has been criticised by the UN, with detention in school as a kind of punishment, where time is again wielded as a weapon by authority. His use of a censored expletive both continues the attempt to appear as an everyday person, as 'one of us', while emphasising the severity of the threat. In fact the true aim appears to be more to scare the audience into submission than to offer fair warning.

4.3 'Time, the wave' and climate change

18 It has been shown that when people try to follow Slessor's third path, of listening to their hearts and acting individually or collectively to shape the future through influencing policy, this can be interpreted as a challenge or even a threat by others, even when such action is sincere and based on well-researched facts; in this instance, the very serious conclusions drawn by climate scientists. Humphries uses irony to claim that the government takes the issue 'deadly seriously': this is not consistent with the following scene, in which government members are **represented** directly, in footage taken at a Pacific Islands leaders' meeting on climate change in 2015. Three Australian ministers, waiting for proceedings to begin, were caught on camera and on microphone in what they believed to be a private conversation:

> PETER DUTTON: Time doesn't mean anything when you're about to have water lapping at your door.

Again Humphries uses direct representation to damn the government in its own words: PM Tony Abbott laughs at Dutton's joke while Morrison represses a smile and looks up at the mic hanging over them. The implication that can be drawn is that they do not take climate science seriously. In Dutton's joke the government is represented as literally laughing at the fatalistic 'Time, the wave', and as discounting the needs of the Pacific Island nations, which are greatly endangered by climate change and which, like students, have a strong stake in the future. For these students at least, time does mean something. Further, they appreciate, as implied in the unkempt orchard of 'Wild Grapes', that in some cases time only overtakes us if we allow it to.

19 The concluding line by Humphries offers another perspective on the government's attitude:

> There is never an excuse for skipping class unless it's a science class in which case we can write you a letter or something.

Again Humphries implies hypocrisy on the government's part: that despite their supposed commitment to the education of Australian youth, they will turn their minds against science if it contradicts their political agenda. The damning implication is that they would even be happy for school students not to be properly educated.

This final paragraph in the body of the essay begins the work of connecting this third section of the essay with earlier themes, of bringing the various strands of the argument together.

For explanations of irony, see the glossary in the English Standard Stage 6 Syllabus, and the Figures of Speech section in Chapter 8 of this book.

The word 'literally' is often used in common speech in a sense that is opposite to its dictionary meaning. If we want to say that a given phenomenon is almost ..., we should say 'virtually', e.g. 'There is virtually no evidence for this common belief'.

Conclusion

Time has a positive side

20 My **understanding** of **human experiences has been deepened by** my study of the prescribed text, which shows that Time and power are very strong influences on experience. However, unlike its representation in 'Out of Time', Time need not be a negative experience. Rather, even though everything passes on eventually, we should seek to make the best use of the time we have, to engage actively, to extract meaning from it and from the experiences that come with it. In 'Gulliver', of the everyday aspects of life that Slessor presents as 'ridiculous manacles', some are negative (hunger and neuralgia) but many could be seen as neutral (hot and cold) or positive (love and sleep). In addition, we have seen that it is also important that writers leave some trace behind of human experiences, just as Slessor did with his experience of being a war correspondent and his life in the colourful environs of Kings Cross.

It is not usual to introduce new material in a conclusion. Here the discussion of 'Gulliver' refers back to earlier discussion of this poem and is an extension of it, so it is appropriate.

Time and the influence of others

21 It has also been shown that influence is often wielded like a weapon by those who have power or authority. Often this takes place through language, which can be used to try to appeal to people, to deceive them or even to 'lash' them, as in Marsden's whip. Again this does not mean that we must expect our experience of society to be always negative.

Rather, the texts considered suggest the conclusion that dialogue and dispute are an integral part of **human experience**. In order for us to engage in such dialogue, Slessor's third mode, of stepping 'out of Time' to listen to the heart and mind, can be the essential step required in promoting a significant wave for change, rather than accepting the passive experience of Time in 'Out of Time', where Time simply passes over us and we bend to it in response. Indeed, not to do so is to risk a more destructive future that would emerge directly out of the inadequacy of humanity's efforts to address global warming, instead of embracing the creative and positive change that can begin to take shape in the human heart and mind.

This final paragraph 'caps off' the essay's argument with a final point that arises logically from the preceding discussion.

Twelve steps in essay writing 'by numbers'

The following twelve steps form a suggested method to help you learn the process of essay writing, but you should be prepared to discover what works best for yourself. This method has been devised with 'take-home', researched essays in mind. Exam essays are discussed in Chapter 9.

1 **Analyse the question.**

Find the keywords: subject, topic, aspect.

2 **Note the 'doing' words.**

3 **Organise data.**

- a Research
- b Assemble
- c Group
- d Rank/order

4 **Develop an argument or theme.**

5 **Plan the essay.**

- The keyhole essay plan
- Other ways of planning: 'mind maps'
- The long walk
- Audition
- The structured response

6 **Draft an introduction.**

  a 'Echo', re-state or paraphrase the question.
  b State your argument.
  c Indicate the key points.
  d (Anticipate your conclusion.)

7 **Check your introduction against the checklist.**

8 **Draft the body of the essay.**

- Treat each topic in turn.
- Sustain your argument.
- Refer back to your argument.
- Give specific 'proofs'.
- Use 'transition' or linking words and phrases.
- Paragraph carefully.
- Qualify your statements.

9 **Draft the conclusion.**

- Re-read the essay question.
- Re-read the introduction.
- Summarise your argument and main points.
- Cap off your argument.

10 **Redraft the essay.**

- Make a fresh start.
- Keep an open mind.

11 **Macro-editing**

- Subtraction
- Addition

12 **Micro-editing**

- Sentence length
- Grammar
- Spelling

Each of the above steps is treated on the following page, in detail. Note that this is a suggested sequence only. It is common to do some of these steps 'out of order' and/or to go back to a particular step to revise or develop something.

Step 1: Analyse the question

Find the keywords: subject, topic, aspect

The importance of answering the question has been emphasised repeatedly. Your first step in doing so is to make sure you understand the question, aided by focusing on keywords. (These are explained in Chapter 4.) Let's look at the sample essay question again:

> Show how study of your prescribed text, and at least one other text, has deepened your understanding of how texts represent human experiences.

Subject keywords: Common module: Texts and Human Experiences

Topic keywords: none specified

Note: This question is very 'open', as it neither supplies particular topics nor specifies a prescribed perspective beyond the broad themes of the syllabus itself. You may well encounter much more closed questions. The following would be a closed version of the above question:

> Show how study of your prescribed text and at least one other text has deepened your understanding of how texts represent human experiences <u>with regard to collective experiences. You should consider at least two of the following themes: human qualities, emotions, language, storytelling and cultures.</u>

Naturally an essay responding to this question with the underlined additions would be quite different to the sample essay.

Aspect Keywords: time, influence, power, authority, heart. These were not specified in the question itself but were supplied as key parts of my argument in response to the question.

Step 2: Note the 'doing' words

In the majority of questions a requirement to perform a particular task is specified in an instruction or 'doing' word. Where this is the case, we must ensure we meet that requirement. In addition, NESA has standardised the use of common instruction words. Some of the most common are reproduced at the end of Chapter 9.

In the sample question we are told to 'show' how understanding is deepened; this doing keyword asks you to demonstrate something. However, it is not enough simply to give examples or point to a few relevant matters. It is also important to explain what they mean and how they support your argument. The best understanding of what you're required to do will always be found in the *context* of the question: that is, in consideration of the question as a whole. Note, however, that not all questions will include instruction words: for example, 'Why would this poem be a good inclusion in an anthology for young Australians?'

Step 3: Organise data

Steps 1 and 2 are concerned with understanding and 'listening to' the question. In Steps 3 and 4 we begin to prepare our detailed answer by re-reading the texts, researching further and then organising the data into manageable sets of notes.

(a) Research

Make a list of research areas before starting your research. For the sample essay, information needed to be researched for four broad themes, which could in turn be divided into smaller subthemes. The initial themes were:

- What is human experience?
- Time
- Kenneth Slessor's career
- Samuel Marsden.

To write this essay I read each poem in the prescribed text several times over and began to take some preliminary notes on their various themes as they relate to human experiences. Other obvious preliminary areas to explore were to understand more about time, to research Slessor's life and career, and to find out about Marsden. Time is a theme often studied in relation to Slessor and one that interests me. You may, however, find very different themes of interest according to how you interpret the Slessor poems.

(b) Assemble

Bring all your notes together, organised in plastic clip folders, manila folders or whichever method you prefer, so you can find the information quickly. It may be worthwhile to create a master list of notes, citing where to find various bits of information. Of course, computer-based notes can be readily filed under different folders and directories, clearly marked so you know where to look for particular information. It is easy to copy information and paste it exactly where you want it, but be very careful to ensure that you reference the source if the data is not your own original work, put all direct quotes in inverted commas and note page references where applicable.

For this essay I had notes on each prescribed Slessor poem, on the Humphries piece and on a number of other texts related to Slessor or the school strike. The most useful of these were then copied and pasted under new headings, based on the different themes I was planning to explore in the essay.

(c) Group

As outlined in Chapter 3, there are different ways of grouping and ordering information. For a question about the themes of a particular work or collection of poems, you would group data under thematic headings. For a question based on the use of language, your headings would relate to various aspects of language.

After researching and thinking about the Slessor poems in relation to my initial four research themes, various related themes emerged: different viewpoints about time, language and power, what is human experience, and ways of persuading. I looked at theories of time in different cultures and found some very interesting material. Only a certain proportion of your notes is likely to appear in the final essay, as only some will be useful in building the argument that eventually emerges out of the research and thinking processes.

Essay notes

Time

'Out of Time': Slessor notes two different forms of time: time the wave and time the knife.

This corresponds to ancient descriptions of time as a river and as an arrow; Slessor refashions this viewpoint. Why?

Time the wave appears gentle, a gently flowing force of nature like the wind and the harbour.

And yet ultimately it destroys everything in its wake, its 'golden undertow'.

Likewise, in 'Wild Grapes' everything passes with time.

However, time the knife is immediately threatening and damaging.

Slessor does not elaborate on this term but it corresponds to the theme of damage and punishment in 'Vesper-Song of Samuel Marsden'. Why?

Australian First Peoples have very different ideas about time compared to Western thinking: the stone calendars of the Wangkumarra people, cyclic time, different seasons to that of Europe. So human experiences of time can vary in different cultures (Gaby and Yunkaporta, 2018).

Also see Duffy (2018): article on conceptions of time in different cultures.

Language and power

Marsden uses language like a whip, with relish.

He seems to take pleasure in the details of convicts' suffering by the lash: 'stripes of jewelled blood'.

Marsden's language likes to emphasise his superior power—'lick and learn at these my boots'—while also pretending to be humble: 'Not mine, the glory'.

He is represented as lacking in Christian forgiveness.

His spiritual qualities are similarly not evident.

What are human experiences?

This needs a good definition to work on: what do we mean by this?

Does everything count as a human experience?

What makes an experience significant?

Is anything significant if it just passes away with time the wave?

Human experiences in the Slessor poems:

- time, like being borne along with the tide
- experiences pass over us, or penetrate us and leave an immediate and lasting effect; the words of others can wound like Marsden's whip
- in 'Gulliver': love, hunger, heat, cold etc.
- cruel treatment of convicts in 'Vesper-Song of Samuel Marsden', Gulliver's cruel predicament
- people have authority or power over our destiny: in 'Beach Burial', 'Gulliver', 'Vesper-Song of Samuel Marsden'
- a less everyday, less go-with-the-flow experience is to take a moment 'out of time', to listen to the heart, and to think critically and creatively about things that matter to us.

The third way in 'Out of Time', of listening to the heart. Is it really 'just a bubble'?

(d) Rank/Order

The final step in organising data is to decide on the sequence in which to discuss topics. Usually we start with the broad picture, the overview, then discuss points in detail, one after the other. There are two levels of ordering or ranking:

1 order of topics
2 ordering points *within* each topic.

As my ideas developed, with respect to how to respond to this question, I narrowed down the range of themes to those finally used in the actual essay. Initially these were time and the influence of those in power and authority. The theme of time in turn was divided into three main strands: time the wave, time the knife and going outside of time. I prioritised the first of these, as Slessor does not have much to say about the second. I based the initial discussion on Slessor's explicit treatment of time in 'Out of Time', before drawing comparisons to some of his other poems. This provided a way of ordering discussion under this heading.

With time the knife, I came to realise that, through the Marsden poem, it could be treated in connection to the second theme, of power and authority's influence on our experiences, so I opted to do this. As the drafting began, further themes emerged: the use of language to persuade, to deceive, to coerce and to punish. This became a subtheme under power/authority.

As my ideas developed I realised that the Humphries piece was a good way both of tackling Slessor's third mode of time—the heart—in more depth, and of connecting it to the theme of authority, so this was a logical topic to put last.

The main organisational principle on which this essay was based, then, was from key theme (time) to second theme, and then connecting the two in the concluding sections.

Step 4: Develop an argument or theme

Now that you have re-read your notes and organised your information, you will have some kind of idea about your response. For a home essay, this idea may change as your writing progresses. For exam essays, you are meant to have explored and tested your thoughts already, although you will have to address this understanding to the specific requirements of the question.

The *argument* or theme should constitute the backbone of your essay, the trunk of your tree. This is how an essay can handle complicated, multi-sided topics in a balanced and orderly way. (The more involved your discussion, the better organised it needs to be, as the sample essay demonstrates.) The argument should be stated early in the essay, referred back to regularly in the body and returned to in the conclusion.

Step 5: Plan the essay

Now you have all the ingredients for an essay, create a rough plan. While it is preferable to plan before writing your first draft, some people simply can't plan until the first draft has been written. For others, a plan is essential before they can even begin to research the essay. You simply need to experiment and find which ways suit you best. You may even find that you can plan some essays but not others.

In the exam room it is essential to do a quick plan so you have at least a rough guide to what you want to say before committing yourself to paper.

Plans, like first drafts, are created for yourself, so they can take any form you find helpful. I discuss two very different kinds below.

The keyhole essay plan

This kind of plan does indeed give you the 'key' to the whole essay. The first part opens onto the main theme. This is followed by the main points that substantiate the argument. Finally, the plan broadens out with a statement of conclusion.

(a) Jot down an 'argument statement'—one or two sentences setting out your main idea.

(b) Follow this with the list of points, noting how they relate to the argument.

(c) Write a concluding statement (if possible).

Keyhole essay plan, Slessor's poems

ARGUMENT STATEMENT

Slessor's poems focus on two key themes that affect human experiences: time and the influence of those with authority or power. Slessor identifies three forms of time—time the wave, time the knife and moments out of time—as important windows on human experience. Although the first and last of these forms are represented initially as pleasant or rich, ultimately all three forms of time appear to bring destruction.

BODY

1. Time the wave in Slessor's poetry: represented initially as pleasant, a gentle force of nature—but ultimately destructive

2. Time the whip and the influence of others: life in the present moment can be oppressive or painful, due in part to the words or actions of others

3. Going 'out of time', listening to the heart: school strike sketch

CONCLUSION

In Slessor's poem it is suggested that the third mode, of going 'out of time', is but a bubble, an illusion. The school strike sketch suggests that it can be employed much more substantially. However, attempts to 'make waves', to not 'go with the flow', may be resisted strongly by those in authority. This suggests that conflict between different points of view is a common theme in human experience.

Other ways of planning: 'mind mapping'

Some writers like to visualise their plan first, literally, so you can draw some kind of diagram if you like. One such method is *mind mapping*. You start this in the centre of the page, writing your theme in the centre of the map. The main branches come next and stem from it directly.

These branches in turn can have branches and sub-branches. You can extend these as far as you like, getting as detailed as you wish.

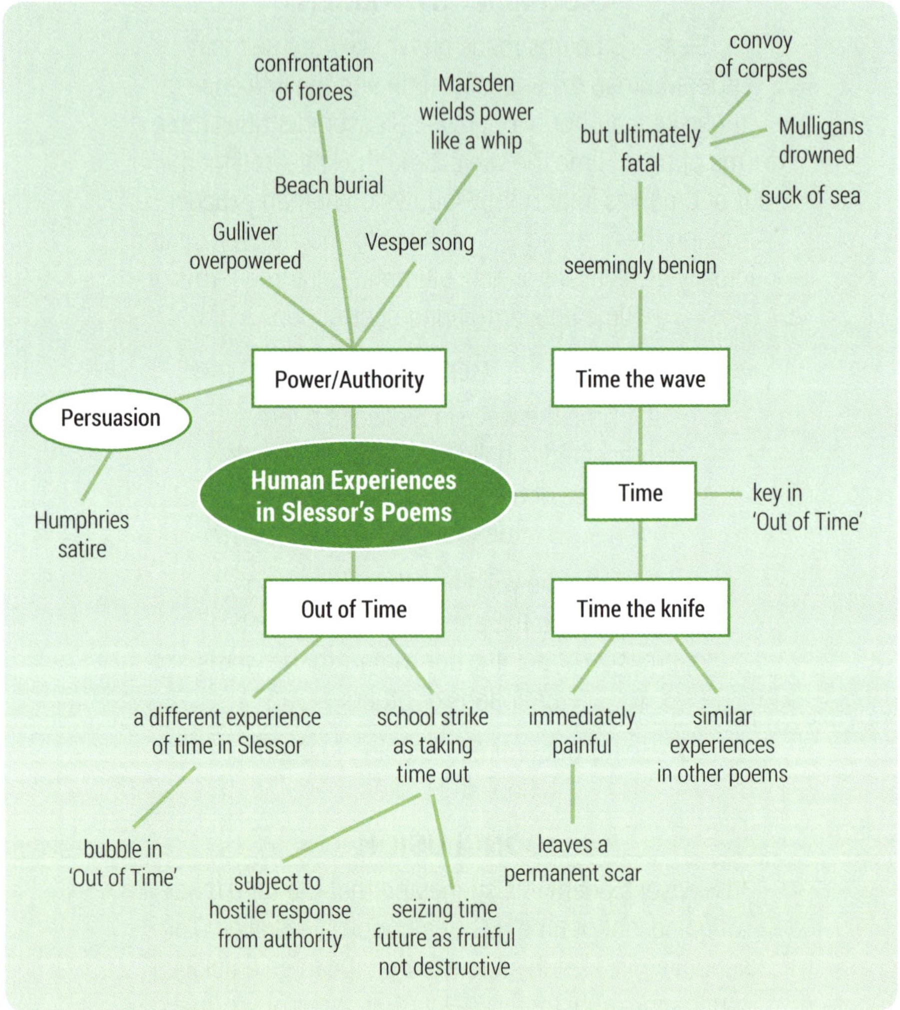

The long walk

Some writers find that going for a long walk, and planning everything in their head, is essential preparation before putting pen to paper. (This is definitely not practical in the exam room, however!)

Audition

You can even start to plan by talking aloud to a friend, or to an audio recorder, such as a smartphone!

The structured response

In the 'structured response' type of question, you must respond to a series of questions in order. This can make planning a lot easier. Even when a structured response question isn't used, sometimes the way the question is written suggests a rough outline:

> *Describe the origins of the Delian League. What was its purpose? How successful was it?*

If you're not an Ancient History student and haven't got the faintest idea what the Delian League was, you can still plan an essay. Even if you think that the Delian League is a basketball competition, you can produce a 'correct' plan, which is useful for guiding your research.

Delian League skeleton essay plan

Introduction:	Explain what the Delian League was and how it arose, *its purpose.*
Success:	(a) Did it achieve its purpose(s)? (b) To what extent? In what ways? (c) Evaluation, overall
Conclusion:	Summarise. Cap off.

Step 6: Draft an introduction

Your introduction has two chief functions:

1 to demonstrate that you have understood the question
2 to state your argument.

You are ready to start your first draft. Many students complain that the hardest thing is to get started. Once begun, you simply have to follow on the same way, and a good introduction is a reference point you can return to if lost. A well-researched essay can still 'run off the rails' very quickly: you might answer a question on the characters in *As You Like It* with a detailed and insightful account of how it would have been staged in Shakespeare's time. Wrong!

In exams, it's even more crucial to 'stay on track' because every moment you spend on something irrelevant is time and space lost for material that could earn you marks. In many HSC subjects you will get very little consideration for answers that are off the point. So let's get this introduction right on track.

One way to picture your introduction is as a kind of 'curtain speech'.

Think of an old-style drama theatre—you've no doubt seen them in films. There's a grand, plush curtain hiding the stage from us. The houselights dim, and in the dark a spotlight shoots out: the announcer strolls into the light and gives a brief speech telling us what treats are in store tonight, in order of appearance. Thunderous applause, the curtains go up and the show begins.

Your introduction is a 'curtain speech': you *don't* launch straight into the 'main act'. First, prepare your audience, the reader; get them settled in, let them know what to expect. Only in following paragraphs do you 'raise the curtain' and start discussing your topics in detail. In the 'curtain speech', announce the main ideas but don't give away all the surprises.

The piece of advice allegedly given by a successful preacher in the United States is often repeated. Asked the secret of his success, he replied something like this: 'First I tell them what I'm going to say. Then I say it. Then I tell them what I just said'. Introduction, body, conclusion. Your reader will appreciate the courtesy.

(a) 'Echo' the question

Consider your poor teachers and examiners. Reading a pile of essays can become tedious and difficult when the writer does not 'signpost'. It is extremely easy to forget something that seems so obvious. It is not enough just to know what you are trying to say or do: it's your job to *communicate*. You can only earn marks for what's in your essay, not what was in your head.

Use the keywords in your introduction. (See the sample essay.) This doesn't mean that you have to rewrite or to parrot the question, which examiners may find annoying. 'Echoing' has two main advantages:

- The reader can 'tune in' quickly and read with greater ease.
- It shows that you are organised, familiar with the formal essay structure and that you understand the question.

(b) State your argument

Having demonstrated that you've understood the question, now indicate the argument you are making in response.

(c) Indicate the key points

A mere mention is sufficient at this stage.

> **TIP:** Even when the 'doing' words of the essay question don't ask you to 'define', it can be a very good idea to define any keywords that may be unclear—both for your benefit and that of the reader, who may not be sure what you mean by it. For example, a word like 'destiny' will mean something to you, but can you define it adequately? In some subjects, you'll need to go beyond everyday dictionaries to find good definitions of specialised terms.

(d) Anticipate the conclusion (optional, advanced)

You can go one step beyond stating your initial argument, by indicating your conclusion. (I have done so in the sample essay.)

Step 7: Check your introduction against the checklist

There is a checklist at the end of this chapter. Try to read your introduction objectively, or ask someone else to check it. If it matches the relevant items, you've laid the foundations for the entire essay. If not, try to fix this up before proceeding. The words don't have to be perfect but the direction should be clear.

Step 8: Draft the body of the essay

As we've said, the hardest thing is to 'get going'. But don't forget, when drafting the body of the essay:

- Treat each topic in turn.
- Sustain your argument.
- Refer back to your thesis.
- Give specific 'proofs'.
- Use 'transition' or linking words and phrases.
- Paragraph carefully.
- Qualify your statements.

Treat each topic in turn

If you have listed your topics or points in the introduction, it's usual to discuss them in the order of listing. This makes it easier to follow the argument.

Sustain your argument

One of the most common weaknesses in student essays is the lack of topic sentences. It's annoying to read a paragraph of discussion with no obvious focus. Don't forget what you're setting out to prove, and don't forget to point out how your discussion supports your case.

If you lose track of your argument, try writing a topic sentence for that paragraph. It's a good practice to write a topic sentence at the start of each paragraph, until topic sentences become a habit.

Refer back to your argument

Keep returning to your theme. You can avoid restating your argument in full, just by concentrating on keywords.

Give specific 'proofs'

Assertions (statements of fact) are very weak if not supported by evidence. Unless what you're saying is definitely well known or quite obvious it's better to give details or reasons. (There is no need to prove that there is such a thing as gravity, for instance!). There are many kinds of 'proof': quotes, examples, statistics, use of language, events, the opinions of critics, historians or economists, and so on.

Use 'transition' or linking words and phrases

See Chapter 4.

Paragraph carefully

See Chapter 4.

Qualify your statements (advanced skill)

'Qualifying' does not come naturally to us. To 'qualify' means to evaluate or give an opinion rather more carefully than you might initially feel inclined to. It is the opposite of being too simplistic or of making sweeping statements about something. Instead of saying that 'Australian writers should write about Australia', reflect that they might also write about overseas experiences or events. Avoid statements beginning with 'Everybody knows that' or 'All ...' unless you are quite sure of what you're saying.

Consider the weaknesses of your argument before someone else does. Just because your argument has weak points doesn't mean it's invalid, only that (like all things) it has its limits. The ability to consider arguments contrary to your own is actually an impressive skill, well worth developing. The ability to see fine 'shades of grey' is evidence of a perceptive, analytical approach.

Step 9: Draft the conclusion

- Re-read the essay question.
- Re-read the introduction.
- Summarise your argument and main points.
- Cap off your argument.

An impressive conclusion can sometimes make the difference between an average essay and a very good one. Many students seem to have the idea that so long as the introduction and conclusion are okay, then the bits in between are just to fill up pages. They might also think that the conclusion is 'basically a summary' and that's all. Wrong on both counts!

Although a conclusion will often start with a brief summary, the best essays go beyond this. This is the hardest essay-writing skill to teach, but one worth developing when you get more confident. I will at least describe the general idea. Your conclusion, by the way, does not have to be limited to one paragraph. It can run to two or more. The same goes for introductions. Suit length to the nature of your essay: the bulk of the essay must always be the body.

You must refer back to the introduction and remind us of what we set out to 'analyse', 'discover', 'discuss', 'compare' or 'describe' (for example). So you will again use the keywords.

Finally, don't forget that question 'So what?'. Your conclusion can make further assessments or comparisons, take the argument further or point to its implications. To cap it off in some way makes a valuable final impression and may give you an edge. (The sample essay goes beyond simply answering the question about human experiences in relation to the prescribed text, in developing the discussion of time into insights about conflict and the importance of engaging actively with time, not necessarily just going with the flow.)

Some possible 'stings in the tail' are:

- a further consequence of the argument
- relating the conclusion to a wider context:
  - implications for the author or character
  - implications for other works by this author

- implications for our understanding of (say) other themes, characters, scenes, and so on
- referring to an outside opinion or author.

Step 10: Redraft the essay

As noted above, in your first draft the attention is on ideas and facts, on developing your argument, rather than on the words used. All first drafts tend to be 'writer-based': they might make perfect sense to ourselves, but not necessarily to others yet. In the second draft you must first check the structure, the organisation, and the clarity of your argument and concepts before worrying about the use of language. The job of translating that draft into a reader-friendly essay begins.

Make a fresh start

It is quite difficult to read our own writing objectively, as if we were some other reader. But if you've been well organised, and managed to write an early first draft, you can put it away for a couple of days or so, then read it back with fresh eyes (the same principle applies to any later drafts too, if you have the luxury of time). Imagine that someone else wrote it, and try to read the draft 'objectively': take note of your immediate reactions when you read, because they will often guide you as to what is working and what isn't. Remember that your role is to encourage this writer, so concentrate more on the strong parts than on the weaknesses! The worst thing you can do to this poor person is to simply dismiss their work; your criticism must be constructive and based on objective questions:

- Is the main argument clear?
- Does there seem to be a point to this essay?
- Are the ideas backed up with evidence?
- Does it actually say what you think it should be saying?
- Do you find it hard to understand what it is saying?

Keep an open mind

An American writing theorist, William Zinsser, has described a 'writing to learn' approach in a book of the same name, based on the idea that in the process of writing you learn by developing your ideas and gaining a truer and deeper understanding. Keep an open mind: above all, it is your job to write a good essay. If it ends up saying what you had wanted it to say, well and good. But be prepared to let it take on a shape of its own if this will be a more accurate, clearer or better argued essay.

If stuck, look again at the data you have collected and organised: What do the facts themselves 'say' to you? What conclusions do they suggest? In most subjects other than English, this approach is automatic, but even in English, the argument you choose should come from the evidence. Sometimes it's easier to base your response on the information you do have than to search for facts to support the argument you wanted to develop. And if you can't find much supporting evidence, this suggests you need to reconsider anyway!

Step 11: Macro-editing

There are two main processes of editing: taking away what does not belong to the essay and adding whatever else is needed.

Subtraction

Imagine a painting of Sydney Harbour. All the usual beauties are there: Opera House, Harbour Bridge, Circular Quay and ... Mount Kosciusko. The mountain touches the whole scene off beautifully—it's well painted and looks great there. Take it away, it doesn't belong. Likewise, take away the bits in your essay that have no relevance: they stand out a mile, they look silly and they'll only lead you astray! It's often tempting to use a favourite quote, to retell the story or discuss your pet obsession in detail, but leave it out unless it advances your argument in some way.

Addition

It's easier to discover what an essay doesn't need than what it does, but with practice you can develop this skill. A good start is to test whether or not you are supporting each assertion. And if you have 'proved' it sufficiently, have you told us why it matters? So what?

You might, for example, be exploring the social and historical context of a prescribed text such as *Stasiland*. This might entail some research about modern European history, about communism and the Cold War, and so on. Then finally, furnish some consequence or result: 'So what?'. For example, what do the stories of various characters in *Stasiland* tell us about human needs and the human spirit?

It has already been mentioned that some students run out of points to make and spend a lot of space just restating their argument. A better strategy is to extend your 'tree trunk' further, or to add new branches.

Some additions that may be appropriate are:

- a quote to support an assertion
- inserting a topic sentence where a paragraph has none
- links between paragraphs
- capping off any paragraph topic, sub-point, or conclusion
- discussing in greater detail.

Step 12: Micro-editing

When you are reasonably happy with the structure and argument, you should work on improving the language. Many writers find that they keep making improvements to various parts of the essay right up to the final draft. However, in the final draft, your focus will probably be on fine tuning. Below, I discuss a few hints and pointers relating to some of the most common problems.

But be warned: it *is* possible to get very neurotic over an essay and to be unable to 'let it go'. If you find you can't bring yourself to stop fiddling with the final draft call your mentor immediately. Tell them it's an emergency! One way of guarding against this danger is to self-evaluate: how many changes did I make in that last redraft? Are they definitely improvements? Why? How important were they? Would they be likely to affect my mark?

Sentence length

I am occasionally asked how long sentences or paragraphs should be. The answer to both questions is 'as long as they need to be'. The most common problem with long sentences is that the writer is trying to cram in too many points. Sometimes they are trying to express several ideas in the one sentence! When in doubt, stick to one main idea per sentence and treat related material in following sentences.

Many of you will be using a grammar checker with your word-processing program. This can be a helpful source of suggestions but do realise that your own brain is far more powerful than any computer, and most programs rely only on certain guidelines which cannot cover all circumstances and issues. The final decision must always rest with you—certainly don't believe everything your computer tells you. There is no grammatical rule about the length of sentences!

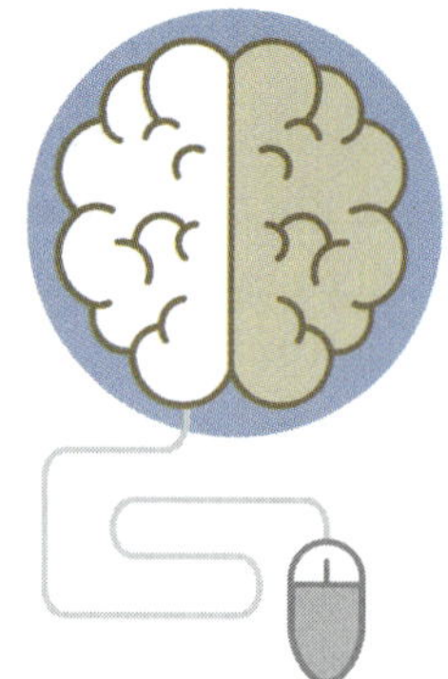

On the other hand. Sentences can be too short. This is a problem. Try linking phrases together into longer sentences like this one, instead of writing something like 'Try linking phrases. Together they can make longer sentences.'

A worse crime, and an extremely common one, is the 'run-on sentence'. You should finish a sentence where the thought ends instead of just keeping it going forever even if the thought is quite complete some people just let those words keep flowing on. (And I hope you can see where a full stop should go in the previous sentence!)

Grammar

With grammar, spelling and punctuation, we tend to repeat our mistakes over and over again. Take careful note of all feedback marked on your essays: this is valuable information that should help you strengthen your writing. Make sure you understand why each mark was made and if in doubt, ask your teacher for clarification.

Spelling

Good spelling is impressive and spelling skills will always be a valuable asset to you, if only to save you embarrassment! Spelling is essentially a memory skill, and as discussed in Chapter 7, the basis of good memory is good organisation and study.

There are a few rules about spelling in English, but because our language is a hybrid of many different languages there are so many exceptions to these rules that they only have limited applicability. One that you certainly should know, however, since so many people have problems here, is 'i' before 'e' except after 'c'. This will help you spell 'believe' correctly, 'receive' and many other frequently misspelt words.

Make lists of words you have misspelt and ask someone to test you occasionally. See how many words you can cross off your list by getting them right three times in a row!

One memory trick you can use is to say the word aloud as it is spelt, rather than how it's meant to sound. How would you pronounce the word 'sword' for instance? Another way of remembering is by creating some image or saying, for example, 'There are too many *o*s in the word *too*.'

I've had students tell me smugly that IBM or 'Mac' do all their spelling for them, 'butt eye due knot no foreshore weather spell chequers ah all ways ewes full. Dew yew? Sum wood say their nigh the hear gnaw they're.' Also, American software can have unreliable ideas about Australian spelling.

Essay editing checklist

Overall

- Writer-based or reader-based?
- Is there a clear argument?
- Is this material relevant?
- What further information is needed?
- Is this statement backed up with evidence?
- Is there an organisational principle ordering the points discussed?
- Is the wording clear? (Try it out on someone else.)
- How can I express this more clearly?

A: Introduction

- Demonstrates an understanding of the question
- States the argument
- Indicates what topics/points will be discussed
- (Optional) Anticipates the conclusion

B: Body

- Paragraphed
- Transitions from paragraph to paragraph
- Topics treated in order

- Argument sustained
- Refers back to argument
- Detailed, specific 'proofs'
- 'Signposted'
- Statements qualified

C: Conclusion

- Initial summary
- Follows on from
  - (a) thesis
  - (b) points made
- Capped off: consequences/extra points are observed

D: Final draft

- Word choice
- Sentence construction
- Grammar
- Neat presentation: typed or word processed if possible
- Spelling

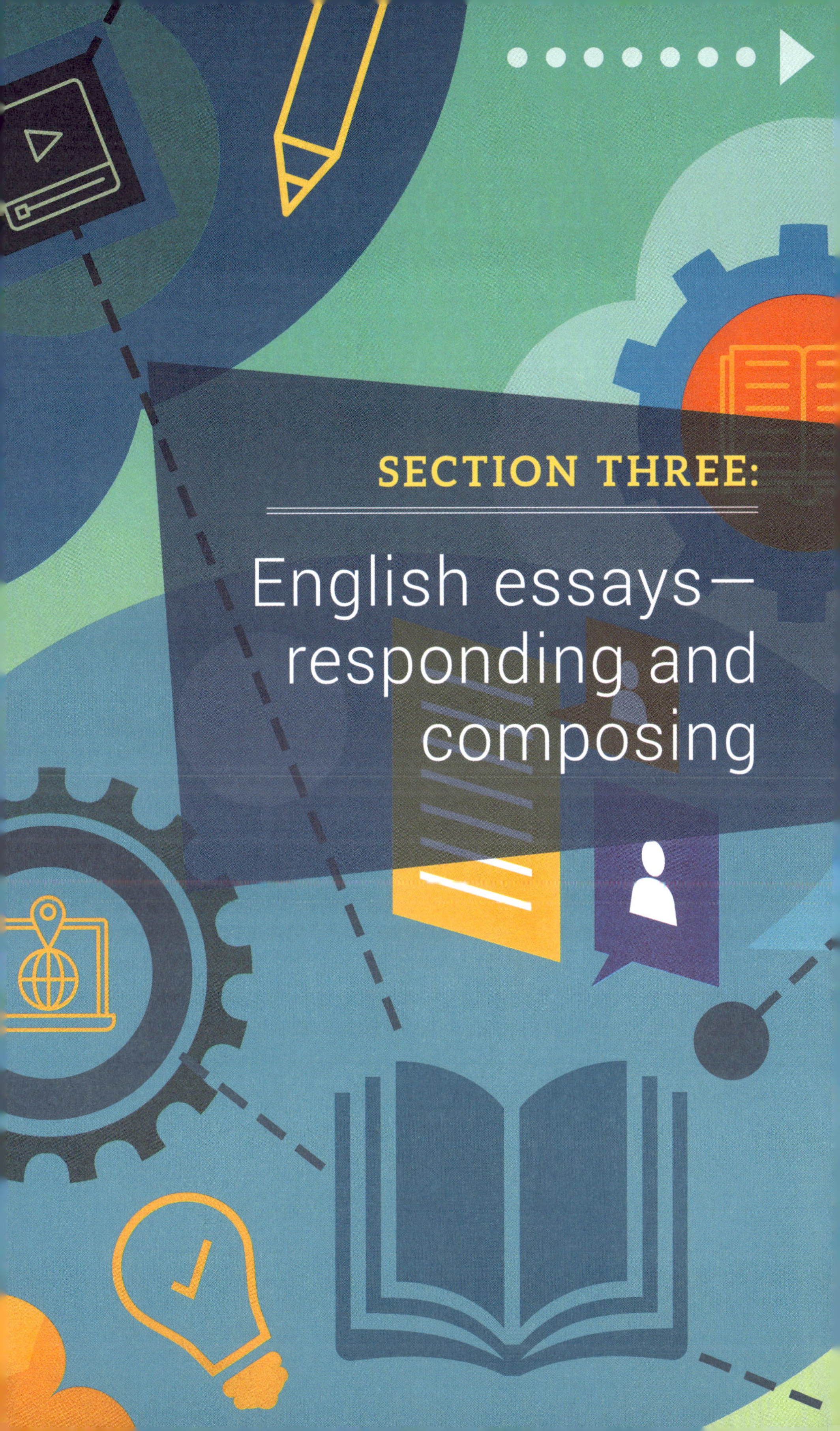

SECTION THREE:

English essays—responding and composing

7 English essays: texts, contexts and the garden of thoughts

Students have often complained to me that with English, unlike every other subject, they don't feel they know what the examiners 'really want' or even how to go about studying it. The approach I outline in this chapter gives you practice with essay writing at the same time as it helps you study for English in an organised fashion.

I remember, when I was young, an older brother proclaiming that his HSC English exams were 'easy'. 'I'd already written my answers in advance' he said. This puzzled me greatly. How *could* he write an essay without knowing what the question was? Impossible! (And, by the way, highly undesirable. Examiners call this trick the 'prepared response', are on guard against it, and treat it ruthlessly. A 'prepared response' either doesn't answer the question, or makes a quick attempt at relating the prepared essay to the question, which generally has very little to do with it.) Obviously my very successful brother hadn't done *that*. So what did he do?

English appears different to most other HSC subjects because there is far less emphasis on 'having the right answer'. This leads some students to the false impression that 'anything goes'. In fact, the best essays in English are the result of careful study and preparation. Even without knowing what question you'll be asked, you can still prepare by developing your own ideas in response to the syllabus requirements. This is your best preparation; and that, I suppose, is what my brother meant.

The best way to prepare for English exams is to write essays: this makes you organise your notes, test and develop your ideas, and read for a purpose. For this reason, I encourage students to base their English study on what I call 'thesis essays'. I'll explain that after first discussing key syllabus requirements.

The Stage 6 English Syllabus

In Mathematics or Science, most of the time, answers are considered to be either objectively right or wrong. In English, one thousand students will write one thousand different answers, all of which can be 'right'. That doesn't necessarily mean that one answer is as good as another; a more helpful distinction is between answers that are well argued and those that are less well argued. In theory, you can furnish any reasonable response you like, so long as it's supported by evidence.

Students are assessed not just on their ideas and knowledge but on how they develop and express them.

It is worthwhile to read the Stage 6 English Syllabus and the syllabus for whichever English course(s) you are studying. These can be found on the NESA website. You will discover that *meaning* is at the heart of English study, and that this is 'achieved through responding and composing'.

That is, you read and study different *texts* (which can include films, multimedia, non-fiction, photographs, paintings, etc.) and formulate a response, which often involves composing an essay. Meaning is not found solely in one text, but between a variety of texts. That is why the syllabus is designed to encourage broad reading of a number of texts and a variety of types of texts.

For example, the sample essay in Chapter 6 compares Slessor's depiction of different forms of time to a satire that touches upon a contrasting approach. To understand the meaning and the various allusions in the satire, one in turn has to understand what the student strike was and what motivated it, through various news reports or commentaries in the media. Texts always take on meaning in context: one way to remember the meaning of this word is to think of it as the facts and circumstances that are related to and that 'go with' the text. The prefix *con* means 'with', as in *connotation*: further implications that go with a given word or phrase. Further useful perspectives could have been found in texts about conceptions of time, for example.

Another key objective of the syllabus is the study of language itself, and some useful terms are discussed in the following chapter, which is devoted just to language.

Just as an argument is the backbone of most essays, your response to an English text becomes the basis for an argument and the backbone of your English essay. An idea based on your response to a text can be called a *thesis*, and can be developed into a thesis essay.

Developing your individual response

Draft a quick essay straight after first reading the text, or viewing the drama, film or other text.

Shakespeare's tragic character Hamlet had some melancholy things to say about the world, complaining that it seemed to him a 'sterile promontory', a rank 'unweeded garden that grows to seed'. It is easy for your study to become a desert, for your own ideas to wither and die, owing to neglect by starvation, thirst and general lack of attention. On the other hand, the garden in which your ideas grow can become overgrown with unruly weeds.

The key to English essays is nurturing your best ideas, developing them and weeding out the failures. This process should begin from the moment you first read your English texts. In developing your individual response, you are encouraged to explore the world past and present, through words; other worlds, now and then, and the great issues facing us today. English can entertain, amuse, inspire, broaden your mind, fascinate and inform; it can change your life forever. For some of you it is the most enriching study you will ever do—even if you don't realise that now. So while slaving over those books, don't forget to stop and enjoy what you're doing, once in a while at least!

First experience of a text

- Do your first reading of the text quickly, then briefly summarise.
- Keep note of your first impressions of a text so as to be able to compare how your perceptions change over time.
- Read the text thoroughly and review and expand on your summary.
- Draft a quick essay based on your ideas.

Your individual response begins with your initial response, so take notes from the moment you read or experience an English *text* (including multimedia, internet, films, etc.). Keep a journal of your reactions, take notes as you read chapter by chapter, poem by poem, or scene by scene: consider key concerns such as main characters, events, setting in time and place, etc. (For stage and audiovisual texts, similar ideas apply to the production itself.)

Keep asking yourself questions: What is this text about? What is going to happen? Who are the main characters? What are they really like? What are we learning about them? Why does the book start at this point? When you record your answers on an ongoing basis, an initial impression will often be contradicted by a later one: this can be valuable for your notes.

It is a good idea to make a very quick first reading without taking any notes. You should write about the book as soon as you have finished reading it, and record your initial impressions. Then re-read more slowly, taking notes as you go.

If you do prefer the slow reading first, don't let yourself get bogged down at a passage or chapter that is unclear to you. Mark the place with a Post-it note or bookmark, and come back to it after finishing the text. Very often the passage will now make sense to you. If not, ask a teacher, parent or other informed source. Soon after having finished reading, summarise the work in terms of the main characters, setting, story, themes, and so on.

The next step is to write a first essay about that work. This will help you organise your thoughts and start weeding out the vague, half-expressed ideas, while nurturing the stronger ideas. You can follow the method set out below in 'A method for writing thesis essays'. Not only does this give you practice with essay writing but it also provides a very solid foundation for your later study effort on that text.

Writing and memory

Many students complain that they can never remember anything about a work several weeks after having read it. This doesn't mean they have a 'bad memory', only that they haven't organised themselves to remember. Anyone who can remember their own name, telephone number and how to drive a car has a perfectly good memory: it's just that they're not using it for specific study purposes yet! As I have said, the key to memory is *organisation*, and good recall is therefore *created* by active study and organisation of thoughts.

One way to remember the 'big picture' is to write about the subject. Unless your first reading and later study are accompanied by note-taking and summaries, you'll forget far too much. Being organised from the start will give you much firmer study foundations to build on.

Computer users know that to prevent their files or documents being lost forever when they turn the computers off, they have to create an appropriate file name, and save this file in an appropriate folder or directory where they'll be able to find it easily. So too must you 'save' your ideas in your own memory: instead of giving them a 'filename' though, you write summaries and brief descriptions to prevent your knowledge being lost. Keep your loose leaves in separate folders for each English text.

Second reading

It's important to read or otherwise engage with a text at least twice, and poems often need to be read several times, since they can be quite elusive at first. Almost like a problem or puzzle, you may need to 'work them out' for yourself. Many students, faced with a class assignment to write, find that re-reading the text without any particular purpose in mind is an excellent way of putting off writing! I have a better suggestion though: if you really have to 'put it off', go out and enjoy yourself. Come back refreshed and ready to really work!

Don't do any work without a clear purpose. If you have written the first draft of an essay *before* re-reading, you might surprise yourself by how much you do remember. When in doubt, discuss details from memory, but mark that section of your draft with an asterisk or question mark to remind you to check when you re-read. You will find when you do so that your mind absorbs much more, and picks up most of the missing pieces you couldn't remember. Gaps in your memory and understanding, quotes you were looking for but couldn't find, certain events you couldn't remember or weren't clear about, will come into place. You will get a lot more out of it by having a clear purpose, than if you are just re-reading, hoping to discover an answer by magic.

The thesis essay study approach

The two chief requirements of HSC English are:

1. **to develop an individual response to a text or unit of work**
2. **to be able to express it in an organised, well-supported and persuasive manner.**

What is a thesis?

We can use another word to summarise the syllabus requirement of responding to a topic or text. Your individual response is developed into a *thesis*.

The word *thesis* comes from a Greek word meaning 'to put, set'. It is defined in the *Macquarie Dictionary* as 'a proposition laid down or stated, especially one to be discussed and proved or to be maintained against objections'. With English you are meant to 'lay down' or state an argument about a text or unit of work. Students often don't realise that they are supposed to find their own thesis, and waste time wondering what the 'right' answer is.

We have already seen that there are two main kinds of question, open and closed. Re-read the essay question for the sample essay in Chapter 6. This question is quite open. It offers no specific directions and thus throws us back on our own resources. However, you may well encounter relatively closed questions that specify both a topic and specific aspects, as one means of discouraging students from attempting to write a rehearsed, 'prepared response'. The key to preparation for exam questions is to have developed a thesis for each area of study, module or elective you are undertaking. I have had a running bet with students for years, that I could always relate a good thesis to any exam question, no matter how closed it was. And of course, the more open a question is, the easier it is for you to use your thesis as the basis for an answer.

If essays grow like trees, then your thesis is the seed. Having prepared yourself with notes and study, your 'tree' begins with an idea, which you attempt to 'sprout' in writing, using various facts and quotes to support it.

The Thesis Essay Study Method: as soon as you start to study a text or topic, draft a full essay about it, using a 'thesis'—your own response or idea—as an argument.

Advantages of the thesis essay study approach

The thesis essay study approach to English coordinates your notes and summaries by writing a thesis essay on each *topic*. This gives you essential practice in writing, prepares you for class assignments and also provides you with a powerful set of notes.

- It gives you year-long practice in essay writing, so that your writing skills will be well honed by the time you come to exams. You will also have plenty of time to develop your ideas and find good evidence to support them. You will have the luxury of time to spend on revising, checking facts and quotes, re-reading, and so on, instead of the futile panic that many students go through.
- Note-taking and reading are done with a purpose, so you will read actively and take notes more efficiently.
- Instead of being piles of 'junk', your notes will be organised into fully articulated ideas.
- You are focused on developing your individual response.
- You are better prepared for class or home assignments throughout the year. By the time an assignment is given out, you have already started thinking about key issues.

- By exam time, although what you hand in is only a first draft, several drafts of essays have gone into organising and testing your ideas on the subject.
- A thesis essay can be written without an essay question having been assigned.

Features of a good thesis

The thesis essay is little different to any other essay, except that instead of being written in answer to a question, it is you who 'asks the question' and decides on what issues or themes to build the argument with. In the process of drafting your thesis essay you will be testing out different possibilities. Here are some guides to help you evaluate them.

Centrality

A good thesis explores themes that are central to the prescribed text. It throws light on, relates to or explains important aspects of the main characters, events or themes of the work. An argument based solely on sandcastle building in the holiday drama *Away* has almost certainly 'lost the plot'.

Supporting facts

The stronger the thesis, the more evidence we can find to support it—so the more this argument and evidence will tell us about the book. I based my thesis essay on *Nineteen Eighty-Four* on the thesis that difference lies at the heart of human experience. This afforded a useful way to explore the suppressive political nature of Oceania, the effects of this suppression on individuals and the reasons for their revolt. The theme is also sufficiently broad that it could apply to various kinds of questions on this text. Although no thesis is likely to cover every important aspect of a text, it allowed me to cast light on some very central features of *Nineteen Eighty-Four.*

Qualified

We have already talked about 'qualifying' our statements. Likewise, arguments need not be completely 'black and white': the best ones are usually *qualified* in some way. Rather than saying, for example, that '*All* the main characters in *Away* are stunted in their development', you will state your case more carefully: 'Some characters are stunted by mental illness, some by physical illness, some by limited opportunity and some by rigid attitudes. 'Qualifying' simply means taking account of the limitations of any opinion and describing as accurately as possible.

Balanced

It is usually preferable to give both sides of the story, thus demonstrating your ability to think critically, to contrast different aspects, and to see shades of meaning and complexity. As discussed earlier, the word 'essay' originally meant 'to weigh', and it is common for an argument to weigh both sides of an issue before summing up. Well-balanced theses deserve a favourable reaction.

A method for writing thesis essays

- Re-read your notes.
- Brainstorm for ideas.
- Choose the strongest ideas.
- Devise a thesis statement.
- Plan the essay.
- Draft the essay.

As with most essays, the hardest thing is getting started.

1 Re-read your notes

Refresh your memory by reading back over your notes and summaries for the text or topic area. (Computer buffs might consider this a bit like loading up important files into RAM!)

2 Brainstorm

Write down every potential thesis idea you can think of: everything that comes up, no matter how silly it sounds. For the time being, concentrate on generating as many ideas as you can—you can weed out the poor ones later. Why not try brainstorming with a group of friends?

Example: You could base a thesis about Louis Nowra's play *Così* on one or all of the following themes or issues:

- the difference between madness and sanity

- how art reflects life
- the nature and value of fidelity
- political activism versus practical social action
- attitudes to drugs
- how experience changes people
- different perspectives on the same subject
- relationships between men and women.

3 Choose the strongest ideas

You now need to choose one key theme for your thesis. You may link several ideas together for this. Now that you have your list, pick through the points and focus on the best. Some other considerations that will guide you are:

- what you know most about
- what you understand best
- what interests you most
- what you consider most important.

If no particular idea stands out, try out the best one, either by proceeding to write more about it, or perhaps discussing it with a friend or teacher. It may be that there is 'something there', but you have yet to find just what it is. Often, indeed almost always, your main hunch has a lot of potential; it may need extra thought and clarification, but will provide you with that all-important starting point.

4 Devise a thesis statement

Write your idea out in full. (This is your thesis statement.) You should, preferably, expand on it in the 1–2–3 fashion. Here's an example:

(a) (Guess what?) *Così* is a drama all about drama itself, both on stage and off.

(b) (Prove it!) Much of the play is devoted to the development and mounting of an unusual dramatic production, with an unusual cast. But the dramas happening in the everyday lives of its characters are as interesting as the dramas they are portraying on stage.

(c) (So what?) Many of the themes about the nature and purpose of drama can be used to reflect on *Così* itself.

5 Organise data

List all the evidence you can find in support of your thesis, under appropriate headings.

6 Plan the essay

Now plan and draft your essay. Instead of being guided by question keywords, however, you should be guided by your own thesis statement, which forms the basis of your argument.

Sample thesis essay: *Nineteen Eighty-Four*

Below is a condensed sample of a thesis essay. Like the sample essay in Chapter 6 it is not perfect, nor a 'model', but should provide some helpful insights into how to write this kind of essay. Concentrate on observing the development of the essay's argument and the various features of the essay that are discussed in the 'dissected' version that follows.

As this is a thesis essay, there is no question to answer. However, it has been devised to respond to key requirements of the Common module. In planning the essay I explored how human experiences are represented in *Nineteen Eighty-Four,* and other texts, in relation to human qualities, emotions, behaviours and motivations.

First here is a summary of the prescribed text for those readers who are not familiar with it.

Summary of *Nineteen Eighty-Four*

Nineteen Eighty-Four, which was first published in 1948, is George Orwell's grim depiction of a hellish totalitarian world of the future, intended as a satire (Williams, 2007, p. 9) of recent political developments in the Europe of the time, such as fascism (the regimes of Hitler and Mussolini) and the communist government in Russia. The word *totalitarian* is defined in the *Macquarie Dictionary* as a centralised government that neither recognises nor tolerates groups or individuals who have a 'differing opinion'. The world of *Nineteen Eighty-Four* is divided into three chief mega-powers: Oceania, based in England and North America, Eurasia and Eastasia. All of the action of the novel takes place in England, a place now called Airstrip 1. *Nineteen Eighty-Four* depicts an extreme state devoted to almost total surveillance of all those who are Party members by means of telescreens, spying helicopters, citizen informers and Thought Police. Total control of citizens is attempted through controlling and restricting the media, books and all sources of history. The Party even attempts to constrict the language so as to control how people think.

Those who are not Party members are called the 'proles' and although they aren't subject to the same degree of control, they are considered by the Party to be such inferior citizens that they are barely human.

For Winston Smith, a worker at the so-called Department of Truth, life has virtually no meaning. There is little joy in life and very little individual freedom. His distrust and questioning of the official regime and its lies lead to increasing rebellion: he starts to write a diary, has an affair with a young woman called Julia and seeks to join a resistance movement called the Brotherhood. After his inevitable arrest he is brainwashed, tortured and broken. Finally he is reformed into a true conformist.

The Uluru Statement is a document released in the upshot of a First Nations National Constitutional Convention held on Anangu land, where the majority of delegates resolved to call for a 'First Nations voice' (Mackay, 2017). It briefly makes the case for the recognition of First Australians in the Australian Constitution, with a dedicated voice in our parliament, and calls for this agenda to be pursued through a special Makaratta Commission. *Makaratta* is a Yolgnu word meaning 'the coming together after a struggle'.

Sample thesis essay: *Nineteen Eighty-Four*

1 *Nineteen Eighty-Four* demonstrates that individual and collective difference is central to human experience. This essay first demonstrates how in this novel human difference is perceived as a threat, before surveying how it is attacked or suppressed, and the effects of this on the individual. These themes are explored in relation to a contrasting document that pursues the opposite agenda; that is, of embracing difference. The focus of the Uluru Statement (McKay, 2017), issued by Australian First Nations people, is the importance of Australia understanding and engaging with First Nations history and culture. More detailed illustration is drawn from the television documentary series *First Australians* (Perkins, 2008). An especially dire aspect of the world of *Nineteen Eighty-Four*, Orwell suggests, is that suppressing individual and collective difference dehumanises us, denies our human

potential for happiness and fulfilment, and makes our lives false and inauthentic. The Uluru Statement further suggests that difference lies at the heart of human experiences and is not something to be merely tolerated but rather to be celebrated and embraced.

2 In Australia we are used to having a high degree of individual freedom. We can express and explore our difference in various ways, including life and career choices, leisure activities, and so on. Orwell's Oceania, however, is obsessed with stamping out human diversity in all its forms because difference is perceived as a threat. This suppression is expressed strenuously through demands for compliance not only in actions and words but also in thoughts and beliefs, and is enforced through an extreme level of surveillance that extends even to the very personal dimensions of home and family life, and of the individual mind. Thus, as the narration notes, it is not the surveillance helicopters that are the biggest problem but the Thought Police (p. 6).

3 Language is one of the more extreme examples of this pressure for conformity. It is deemed important for comrades to not only take an interest in news bulletins about economic productivity and to express enthusiasm for a supposed increase in the chocolate ration (even when in reality it is a reduction) but also to express this only in the approved language ('double plus good'). As the Appendix explains, Newspeak has the ultimate aim, as the language is increasingly refined and reduced, of making it impossible to think thoughts that differ from orthodox thinking (p. 241; see also p. 45). This further demonstrates the extent to which difference is perceived as a threat.

4 Party members are encouraged not merely to comply with Party rules and thoughts, but also to distrust difference in others. In *Nineteen Eighty-Four* difference is attacked and suppressed in many ways. Within Oceania the two greatest targets are the revolutionary Goldstein and the supposed subversive movement the Brotherhood, key targets that are demonised during the regular Two Minutes Hate and in Hate Week. Externally, whichever state Oceania is supposedly at war with is also a focus. The purpose of this focus on hate appears to be to coerce the people to unite in one cause, to blame their own rage and frustration at their hollow lives upon others whose real crime, if any, is in disagreeing with the Party. For example, Julia considers that:

> the sex instinct created a world of its own which was outside the Party's control and which therefore had to be destroyed if possible. What was more important was that sexual privation

induced hysteria, which was desirable because it could be transformed into war fever and leader worship. (p. 109)

5 These targets also serve another purpose: not merely to unite every individual to the Party line in a frenzy of anger and shouting but also to serve as a deterrent warning of what to expect for any individual who may feel drawn to deviating from the official values. The spectacle of public hangings is the most dramatic expression of this demonising of difference, and even children are encouraged to attend them.

6 This official value of hating human difference is represented as having dehumanising effects on those subjected to it; for example, by suppressing their compassion. In an early scene Winston records in his diary, with apparent approval, even relish, having seen a newsreel movie featuring bloody scenes in which helpless refugees are attacked by guns from a helicopter. Further, it is later noted that Winston 'disliked nearly all women' (p. 12). Even in relation to Julia, with whom he will have an affair, early in the novel Winston entertains violent fantasies about her despite her youth and attractiveness. These are partly motivated by another effect of this climate of distrust of others: his fear that she may secretly work for the Thought Police. This leads to his applying a form of Doublethink to her: hating her because she is beautiful and because he finds her attractive. This too is dehumanising in denying his true reality.

7 As O'Brien notes, the sole agenda of the Party is power. The Party seeks to retain seemingly absolute power by isolating and enfeebling the individual in order to ensure that no-one can trust anyone else. Personal relations are a threat as they make people happier and less dependent on the state, and can even lead to forming significant groups. For this reason the Party attacks social units such as the family, encouraging family members and friends to spy on each other. Likewise, friendships are tainted with paranoia and people's leisure time activities are structured for them in order to stop the development of authentic, nurturing relations. Because of this, Winston's affair with Julia appears to be a 'rebellion', a threat to the state, as 'Desire was thoughtcrime' (p. 58).

8 The principal effect of this suppression of difference, however, is in stimulating resistance in the individual. Resistance in various forms is a dominant theme in the narrative. It begins with Winston beginning to write a diary, which soon develops into writing rebellious phrases and then avoiding Party-approved leisure activities, exploring parts of London he is not supposed to visit, and beginning an affair with Julia.

Especially through this relationship he begins to discover some of the humble, beautiful experiences that life can offer, in simple matters like the feeling of putting his arm around Julia's waist, having a small piece of real chocolate and the sound of a thrush singing in the sun: these experiences offer the hope of Winston rediscovering his humanity. Julia's resistance is more strategic as it is protected by her own creative use of Doublethink. She is a very active member of the Anti-Sex League since the Party insists that sex is solely for reproduction and not for pleasure. At the same time she pursues a very active and unorthodox sex life.

9 A consequence of this regime attacking human difference is that the individual ends up facing a dilemma: either to comply fully and survive, at the cost of dehumanisation and living in frustration and fear, or to pursue one's own path and run the extreme risk of detection, torture and death. However, some forms of resistance appear to be unconscious or instinctual, and thus extremely hard to control.

> Your worst enemy, he reflected, was your own nervous system. At any moment the tension inside you was liable to translate itself into some visible symptom. He thought of a man whom he had passed in the street a few weeks back … They were a few metres apart when the left side of the man's face was suddenly contorted by a sort of spasm … it was only a twitch, a quiver, rapid as the clicking of a camera shutter, but obviously habitual. He remembered thinking at the time: That poor devil is done for … The most deadly danger of all was talking in your sleep. (p. 29)

Thus even the supposedly easier path of complete compliance is in reality very difficult because the urge to express one's true nature is so strong. The suppression of human difference causes deep individual suffering.

10 Perhaps the most powerful form of individual resistance in *Nineteen Eighty-Four* is Winston's drive to find the truth. This is expressed in his desire to piece together his memory, to try to restore lost fragments, even though he knows that, if his memory differs from official state accounts, he is a thought criminal. In his isolation he cannot share or compare his memories and experience with anyone; for example, his memory of seeing a photograph confirming that the confessions of Rutherford and others had been false is dangerous, and he chooses to conform by sending the photograph to the 'memory hole' to be destroyed. Although

he has become used to lies and cover ups he feels the loss of this photograph particularly keenly:

> But this was concrete evidence; it was a fragment of the abolished past, like a fossil bone which turns up in the wrong stratum and destroys a geological theory. It was enough to blow the Party to atoms, if in some way it could have been published to the world and its significance made known. (p. 36)

What gives that photograph such power is that it is true, in a world built on falsehoods.

11 This memory is important to him because it offers some hope of basing his thoughts and values on objective truth. Likewise, a diary is a means of keeping a permanent record of one's experience in order to provide an independent reference point against the ever-changing stories and lies of Big Brother. Winston's need for a concrete and objective record is symbolised by his attraction to buying the coral paperweight, which in itself bears witness to a previous time:

> It's a little chunk of history that they've forgotten to alter. It's a message from a hundred years ago, if one knew how to read it. (p. 119)

The purpose of a paperweight is to prevent papers from being blown away and lost. This contrasts starkly to Winston's job in the Department of Truth, where he is always destroying documents and photos from the past. Likewise, his memory of nursery rhymes is just fragments. Although apparently trivial in themselves these songs are important because they are historical texts, not the fake products of the Department of Truth: the fake histories and forged photographs, the garbled rewritings of poems now considered offensive, the mechanically composed 'sentimental songs' and poems, and the novels created bureaucratically using a novel-writing machine.

12 However, when it comes to Winston and Julia seeking to engage in active resistance, to join the Brotherhood, just how limited Winston's progress is toward truth becomes apparent: to O'Brien he expresses his willingness to undertake various atrocious acts, such as murdering innocent people, for the cause. Winston has not found an authentic path for himself. He has not developed a considered set of beliefs and values to guide his life. For this reason, the first stage in Winston's new path of resistance is to run the risk of acquiring and reading the Goldstein book, where he finds a 'more powerful, more systematic' (p. 161) and historical

case for the coming revolution 'through the spread of enlightenment' (p. 210). This suggests that credible, well-considered texts have the potential to transform our ideas and values, to guide us toward happier and more authentic human experiences. Thus Winston's early impressions of Goldstein's book are that 'it was bliss, it was eternity' (p. 150); it fascinates and reassures him (p. 161).

13 A chosen short text illuminates the importance of articulating a clear statement of values and aspirations. The Uluru Statement from the Heart (2017), in strong contrast to the intolerance of difference in Oceania, urges the importance of recognising and embracing difference in Australian history and in contemporary society. In particular, it calls for formal recognition of Australia's First Peoples in the Australian Constitution and parliament. In support of this claim it offers a contextualising sketch of the history of our First Peoples, some broad aims and the reasoning behind them, and invites other Australians to join in this cause.

14 This Statement not only calls for the recognition of difference but, in its approach and use of language, seeks to demonstrate how different cultures can co-exist. This is in strong contrast to the insistence on conformity and homogeneity in *Nineteen Eighty-Four.* It begins by offering historical context, with a brief account of the history of the 'first sovereign Nations of the Australian continent'. The language takes in three perspectives: in addition to First Nations culture, it refers to the broader Australian contexts of 'common law' and 'science'. Thus, from the outset, the statement integrates First Nations and Western perspectives. Similarly, it uses a measure that is common in conventional Western thinking—statistics—in noting that 'Proportionally, we are the most incarcerated people on the planet'. This choice of telling detail adds power and persuasiveness to the argument that a great wrong in this country needs to be addressed: 'the torment of our powerlessness'. Thus, unlike *Nineteen Eighty-Four,* in which both history and context are denied, the statement offers an objective and factual foundation for its claims. In stark contrast Winston is finally made to accept that 2 + 2 = 5. Indeed he confronts a situation 'more terrifying than torture or death' (p. 31): a world with no objective context. The blatant Party slogan is to 'control the past' (p. 199) in order to also control the future through systematic lying and fakery.

15 A key element of First Nations difference addressed in this statement is the emphasis on spiritual values: it is noted that the legalistic term 'sovereignty' has a spiritual nature, based on 'ownership of the soil'. This

perspective, stressing the land itself, is in strong contrast to Western practice, in which ownership of the land is expressed in lines drawn on paper and is usually a means of acquiring wealth. In the documentary series *First Australians* (Perkins, 2008) the connection between spirituality and the land is explained in greater detail. The opening sequence of each episode recounts a creation story in which:

> Before the Dreaming all that moved on the land was the wind. Then came life. Giant beings came down from the sky, came from the sea, from within the earth itself. Part-animal, part-human, these beings travelled the land. They danced and made love. They hunted and fought, creating a landscape as they went. In everything they touched they left their essence, their life force, making the land itself sacred to those that would follow them.

This story provides the basis for other parts of the series, in which the sacredness of waterholes, trees, certain locations, geographical features, and so on, is revealed through stories of early contact with white people. In Episode 4 it is explained that for the Arrente desert people of Central Australia, their Dreaming is known through the *Altyerra*, the sacred law that 'leads their life'. Aerial photography of the Caterpillar Ranges, accompanied by a voiceover telling the story of the Caterpillar people who are their ancestors, visually conveys the resemblance of these rock formations to caterpillars. The effect is to bring the landscape alive with meaning through the reader's exposure to this perspective.

16 The difference in spirituality between the colonising peoples and the First Peoples is made apparent in the story of three German missionaries who came to Arrente land from Adelaide. The narrator records that at first, the gifts of flour and sugar were very welcome, but they came at the price of having to wear clothes and to listen to the 'endless German sermons'. It also became clear to the elders, who began to shun the missionaries, 'what their game was: that these people didn't respect their beliefs' (Peter Vallee, in Perkins, 2008). The missionaries apparently did not recognise, nor seek to enquire about, the nature of First Nations spiritual beliefs but instead, aimed to stamp them out. They also misinterpreted the intent when Arrente men and women dressed up and decorated themselves for their dances, fearing they were about to engage in savage rituals and calling them 'heathens'. This word strongly conveys how perceived difference can be used to put down others. Some meanings of this word are 'irreligious', 'unenlightened' and 'barbarous' (the *Macquarie Dictionary*). Ironically, however, in their creation story

the Arrente people already had their equivalent of the book of Genesis, which the missionaries taught them. According to Herman Malbunka, '... the white people wanted to convert them, to change them. They wouldn't change because of what they had learnt. We have our *Twerrenge*'. Similarly to Winston's experience in *Nineteen Eighty-Four*, the individual is resistant to pressures to conform: our difference is an intrinsic part of human experience.

17 The Uluru theme that different cultures can co-exist in mutual respect is reinforced by the story of one of the first Indigenous 'converts', Tjallkabotta, who according to Max Stuart came to be an *Ngkarte*, a 'church leader', both for the Christian church, where he became an evangelist, and for his native kin. In reality, he did not 'convert' (change completely) to Christianity, but adopted an additional system of knowledge, for 'He knew every *Tywerrenge* and never let on' (Max Stuart). By using Indigenous words and concepts, the documentary offers to non-Indigenous viewers the opportunity of likewise adding to their cultural knowledge. *Tywerrenge* are sacred objects, such as stones or wooden tablets, often with totemic markings that convey aspects of the *Altyerra*. According to Stuart, Tjallkabotta was a 'visionary', one who indeed learnt to, in the words of the Uluru Statement, 'walk in two worlds' at once, combining the worlds of the Christian 'god in the sky' and also the law in the land. One marker of his ability to bridge this divide of difference is in his adopting the name 'Moses'. This draws a connection between the biblical figure, who was given his people's law in the tablets with the Ten Commandments, and the native practice of inscribing *Altyerra* on sacred objects. Tjallkabotta understood his native land and culture through its customs and language but was also comfortable living among Europeans and understanding their world, sharing their language and thought.

18 The Uluru Statement's insistence on the spiritual dimension of 'sovereignty' illustrates the importance of articulating one's values and beliefs. In *Nineteen Eighty-Four* even objective common sense is considered 'the heresy of heresies' (p. 68). *Heresy* is a term generally used in relation to religious thought but in Oceania any kind of spiritual principle is denied and the Party defines any unapproved thinking as 'heresy'. This explains the significance of the nursery rhyme 'Oranges and Lemons', which tells what various church bells 'say'. This rhyme dates back to a time when the church had been a living institution, when the bells were rung for a purpose and had meaning. Winston, who has no memory of hearing church bells ring, is dimly aware that there are deeper dimensions to life than the Party pretends.

19 However, the Party, in seeking to eliminate any possibility of heresy, avoids the historical mistake made by states and churches in the past: that is, of making martyrs out of dissenters. O'Brien explains that the example of such martyrs could encourage others. Rather, O'Brien seeks to make minds 'perfect', defined as eliminating all resistance and difference: a complete 'conversion' by torture and brainwashing. As he warns Winston:

> Everything will be dead inside you. Never again will you be capable of love, or friendship, or joy of living, or laughter, or curiosity, or courage, or integrity. You will be hollow. We shall squeeze you empty, and then we shall fill you with ourselves. (p. 206)

20 While the private resistance of Winston and Julia is ultimately futile, another contrasting theme in the Uluru Statement is its call for positive change, to celebrate difference and bridge the divide between the First Nations and the broader community. In contrast to the emphasis in *Nineteen Eighty-Four* on intolerance of all deviation from official values, the Uluru Statement promotes not merely tolerance but appreciation of the potential of difference. The language balances the formal register of 'substantive constitutional change and structural reform' with the more poetic expression of allowing 'this ancient sovereignty [to] shine through as a fuller expression of Australia's nationhood'. Here the figurative expression 'shine through' metonymically implies sunlight and relief from a present state of darkness. This delicately evokes the truth of a negative past while putting the emphasis on a positive future.

21 The language also attempts to bridge the difference divide in other ways by reaching out directly to all Australians: 'We invite you to walk with us in a movement of the Australian people for a better future'. Characterising this as an Australian rather than First Nations movement rhetorically emphasises the need for unity and dialogue. Similarly in the first sentence, rather than listing the different states and regions from which conference delegates came, it refers to what unites them by referring to their 'coming from all points of the southern sky'. This figurative language is a further reminder of First Nations connections to nature, again metonymically conveyed by the 'southern sky', and also evokes the creation story of giants coming from the sky. Likewise, in speaking to a future where 'our children ... will walk in two worlds and their culture will be a gift to our country' it insists both on the continuance and viability of First Nation's culture and its coexistence with the wider community.

22 The grim, inhuman world of *Nineteen Eighty-Four* illustrates that difference is at the heart of human experiences, and demonstrates the importance of expressing and exploring our difference by showing the consequences when others try to suppress it. Difference is inherent to human experiences, in individual values, thoughts, feelings and desires, and in collective forms such as culture and language. It has been shown that suppression of difference adversely affects those it touches.

23 In contrast the Uluru Statement, based on a response to the truth of Australian history, offers a very different perspective: recognising, exploring and embracing difference and seeking to bridge cultures through mutual understanding. It leads by example, employing the formal language of mainstream politics and legislation while incorporating First Nation's cultural values, such as ties to nature and family, and connection to land and language. In a direct address to the reader (via the use of the second person) it continues the metaphor of a journey and a dialogue: 'We invite you to walk with us in a movement of the Australian people'. The word *movement* is a pun, as it refers both to the furtherance of this cause as a movement and to the 'movement' of peoples across the native land in a metaphorical 'trek across this vast country'. Rather than using the imperative form, in saying just 'Walk with us', which would sound like a command, instead it extends an invitation to all Australians ('We invite you') to do so, to engage with and understand the culture of the traditional custodians of the land. Thus it models how difference can be affirmed and celebrated, to create new, better outcomes for that 'fuller expression of Australia's nationhood' in which today's young become 'our hope for the future'. In complete contrast to the hateful persecution of difference in *Nineteen Eighty-Four*, the Uluru Statement suggests that embracing difference can help create a happier society that innovates and flourishes, and which draws on the creative possibilities of human diversity and difference. It stresses what unites us, like the southern sky and the land in which we all live, but which many of us could better appreciate and understand.

References

McKay, D 2017, *Uluru Statement: a quick guide*, Parliament of Australia, retrieved from www.aph.gov.au/About_Parliament/Parliamentary_Departments/Parliamentary_Library/pubs/rp/rp1617/Quick_Guides/UluruStatement

Orwell, G 1970, *Nineteen Eighty-Four*, Harmondsworth, Penguin Books.

Perkins, R 2017, *First Australians*, television documentary series, Episode 4, Blackfella Films.

Uluru Statement from the Heart 2017, Central Land Council, retrieved from www.clc.org.au/index.php?/publications/content/the-uluru-statement

Williams, R 2007, 'Afterword: Nineteen Eighty-Four in Nineteen Eighty-Four', in H Bloom (ed.), *George Orwell's Nineteen Eighty-Four*, New York, Chelsea House.

'Dissected' version of the sample thesis essay

The same essay is now reprinted with notes.

- Headings are inserted, for guidance. These would not be used in the actual essay.
- Paragraphs are numbered.
- The key parts of topic sentences are underlined.
- The thesis statement is double underlined.
- Comments are in *italics*.
- The topic keyword (as provided by myself) is in reverse type.
- Aspect keywords (as provided by myself) are in **bold**.

Because there is no essay question, there are no question keywords. Topic keywords define the main, broad themes of the argument (in this case, the thesis that in my reading of *Nineteen Eighty-Four* difference is central to human experiences). Aspect keywords refer to specific elements of the defined topic: words that relate to key parts of the argument or substantiating claims.

Topic keyword: difference

Aspect keywords and phrases: threat, dehumanising, suppression, resistance, embracing difference, truth

Introduction

1 *Nineteen Eighty-Four* demonstrates that individual and collective difference is central to human experience. This essay first demonstrates how in this novel human difference is perceived as a **threat**, before surveying how it is attacked or **suppressed**, and the effects of this on the individual. These themes are explored in relation to a contrasting document that pursues the opposite agenda; that is, of **embracing difference**. The focus of the Uluru Statement (McKay, 2017), issued by

Australian First Nations people, is the importance of Australia understanding and engaging with First Nations history and culture. More detailed illustration is drawn from the television documentary series *First Australians* (Perkins, 2008). An especially dire aspect of the world of *Nineteen Eighty-Four*, Orwell suggests, is that suppressing individual and collective difference **dehumanises** us, denies our human potential for happiness and fulfilment, and makes our lives false and inauthentic. The Uluru Statement further suggests that difference lies at the heart of human experiences and is not something to be merely tolerated but rather to be celebrated and embraced.

The introduction immediately introduces the topic of my thesis, then proceeds to list related aspects that will be treated. The thesis statement itself comes at the end of the paragraph in this particular essay. Often it would come first.

Nineteen Eighty-Four is synonymous with some contemporary themes that are very pertinent to human experiences today: surveillance, social control, compromised privacy and the misuse of communication technology. At the time of writing, there are obvious applications in the fact that 'fake news' has become a common expression in Western democracies, or in some developments in the Asian region, in which online media have reportedly been used by governments to shame citizens. In this essay I have opted to explore Nineteen Eighty-Four in relation to another aim of the Common Module; that is, of reflecting 'particular lives and cultures' in exploring Australian First Nations culture.

Section 1: Difference in *Nineteen Eighty-Four*

1.1 Difference seen as a threat in *Nineteen Eighty-Four*

2 In Australia we are used to having a high degree of individual freedom. We can express and explore our difference in various ways, including life and career choices, leisure activities, and so on. Orwell's Oceania, however, is obsessed with stamping out human diversity in all its forms because difference is perceived as a **threat**. This **suppression** is expressed strenuously through demands for compliance not only in actions and words but also in thoughts and beliefs, and is enforced through an extreme level of surveillance that extends even to the very personal dimensions of home and family life, and of the individual mind. Thus, as the narration notes, it is not the surveillance helicopters that are the biggest problem but the Thought Police (p. 6).

The first sentence in the above paragraph looks as if the essay has gone 'off topic' as it does not directly address difference as a threat, the theme for the first section of the body. However, it provides important background for the argument that follows and begins to draw the necessary link in the second sentence.

3 Language is one of the more extreme examples of this pressure for conformity. It is deemed important for comrades to not only take an interest in news bulletins about economic productivity and to express enthusiasm for a supposed increase in the chocolate ration (even when in reality it is a reduction) but also to express this only in the approved language ('double plus good'). As the Appendix explains, Newspeak has the ultimate aim, as the language is increasingly refined and reduced, of making it impossible to think thoughts that differ from orthodox thinking (p. 241; see also p. 45). This further demonstrates the extent to which difference is perceived as a **threat**.

After the broad statements of the opening paragraphs the discussion starts to turn to more specific, concrete points, to substantiate them. This pattern is also repeated in later sections.

1.2 Suppression of difference

4 Party members are encouraged not merely to comply with Party rules and thoughts, but also to distrust difference in others. In *Nineteen Eighty-Four* difference is attacked and **suppressed** in many ways. Within Oceania the two greatest targets are the revolutionary Goldstein and the supposed subversive movement the Brotherhood, key targets that are demonised during the regular Two Minutes Hate and in Hate Week. Externally, whichever state Oceania is supposedly at war with is also a focus. The purpose of this focus on hate appears to be to coerce the people to unite in one cause, to blame their own rage and frustration at their hollow lives upon others whose real crime, if any, is in disagreeing with the Party. For example, Julia considers that:

> the sex instinct created a world of its own which was outside the Party's control and which therefore had to be destroyed if possible. What was more important was that sexual privation induced hysteria, which was desirable because it could be transformed into war fever and leader worship. (p. 109)

The indented quote above is called a 'block quote', a form of presentation that is neat, legible and useful for quotes of (say) three to four lines or longer. I have provided a page reference here; generally that is a good idea where one offers actual quotes.

5 These targets also serve another purpose: not merely to unite every individual to the Party line in a frenzy of anger and shouting but also to serve as a deterrent warning of what to expect for any individual who may feel drawn to deviating from the official values. The spectacle of public hangings is the most dramatic expression of this demonising of difference, and even children are encouraged to attend them.

The words 'also serve another purpose' apply the effective technique of offering linking or signposting words near the start of a paragraph. This makes it easier for the reader to follow how the present paragraph relates to the unfolding argument overall.

1.3 Effects of suppressing difference

1.3.1 Dehumanising the individual

6 This official value of hating human difference is represented as having **dehumanising** effects on those subjected to it; for example, by suppressing their compassion. In an early scene Winston records in his diary, with apparent approval, even relish, having seen a newsreel movie featuring bloody scenes in which helpless refugees, are attacked by guns from a helicopter. Indeed, it is later noted that Winston 'disliked nearly all women' (12). Even in relation to Julia, with whom he will have an affair, early in the novel Winston entertains violent fantasies about her despite her youth and attractiveness. These are partly motivated by another effect of this climate of distrust of others: his fear that she may secretly work for the Thought Police. This leads to his applying a form of Doublethink to her: hating her because she is beautiful and because he finds her attractive. This too is dehumanising in denying his **true** reality.

1.3.2 Isolating the individual

7 As O'Brien notes, the sole agenda of the Party is power. The Party seeks to retain seemingly absolute power by isolating and enfeebling the individual in order to ensure that no-one can trust anyone else. Personal relations are a threat as they make people happier and less dependent on the state, and can even lead to forming significant groups. For this reason the Party attacks social units such as the family, encouraging family members and friends to spy on each other. Likewise, friendships are tainted with paranoia and people's leisure time activities are structured for them in order to stop the development of authentic, nurturing relations. Because of this, Winston's affair with Julia appears to be a 'rebellion', a **threat** to the state, as 'Desire was thoughtcrime' (58).

1.4 Stimulating resistance

1.4.1 Everyday resistance

8 The principal effect of this **suppression** of difference, however, is in stimulating **resistance** in the individual. Resistance in various forms is a dominant theme in the narrative. It begins with Winston beginning to write a diary, which soon develops into writing rebellious phrases and then avoiding Party-approved leisure activities, exploring parts of London he is not supposed to visit and beginning an affair with Julia. Especially through this relationship he begins to discover some of the humble, beautiful experiences that life can offer, in simple matters like the feeling of putting his arm around Julia's waist, having a small piece of real chocolate and the sound of a thrush singing in the sun: these experiences offer the hope of Winston rediscovering his humanity. Julia's resistance is more strategic as it is protected by her own creative use of Doublethink. She is a very active member of the Anti-Sex League since the Party insists that sex is solely for reproduction and not for pleasure. At the same time she pursues a very active and unorthodox sex life.

The topic sentence need not always be at the start of the paragraph.

1.4.2 Unconscious resistance

9 A consequence of this regime attacking human difference is that the individual ends up facing a dilemma: either to comply fully and survive, at the cost of **dehumanisation** and living in frustration and fear, or to pursue their own path and run the extreme risk of detection, torture and death. However, some forms of **resistance** appear to be unconscious or instinctual, and thus extremely hard to control.

> Your worst enemy, he reflected, was your own nervous system. At any moment the tension inside you was liable to translate itself into some visible symptom. He thought of a man whom he had passed in the street a few weeks back ... They were a few metres apart when the left side of the man's face was suddenly contorted by a sort of spasm ... it was only a twitch, a quiver, rapid as the clicking of a camera shutter, but obviously habitual. He remembered thinking at the time: That poor devil is done for ... The most deadly danger of all was talking in your sleep. (p. 29)

Thus even the supposedly easier path of complete compliance is in reality very difficult because the urge to express one's **true** nature is so strong. The **suppression** of human difference causes deep individual suffering.

The sentence introducing the quote explains its significance. The sentence immediately following it draws a conclusion from it. These are ways in which a quote is 'interpreted' and integrated into the argument.

This above paragraph is a variant on the 1-2-3 structure. In this case the topic sentence states the theme, which is substantiated in the rest of the paragraph, and then capped off with a mini-conclusion in the last sentence.

The ellipsis, a series of three spaced dots (...), is used to indicate that one has left out part of the original text. It is important to make quotes word perfect and to indicate any changes one has made for the sake of integrity of the text.

1.4.3 Resistance through truth

10 Perhaps the most powerful form of individual **resistance** in *Nineteen Eighty-Four* is Winston's drive to find the **truth**. This is expressed in his desire to piece together his memory, to try to restore lost fragments, even though he knows that, if his memory differs from official state accounts, he is a thought criminal. In his isolation he cannot share or compare his memories and experience with anyone; for example, his memory of seeing a photograph confirming that the confessions of Rutherford and others had been false is dangerous, and he chooses to conform by sending the photograph to the 'memory hole' to be destroyed. Although he has become used to lies and cover ups he feels the loss of this photograph particularly keenly:

> But this was concrete evidence; it was a fragment of the abolished past, like a fossil bone which turns up in the wrong stratum and destroys a geological theory. It was enough to blow the Party to atoms, if in some way it could have been published to the world and its significance made known.
> (p. 36)

What gives that photograph such power is that it is true, in a world built on falsehoods.

A similar pattern to paragraph 9 is used here to interpret the material in the block quote. The use of the word 'isolation' refers us back to the discussion in section 1.3.2, helping to draw the various strands of the argument together.

The opening words of this paragraph 'signpost' that the following discussion announces a key theme.

11 This memory is important to him because it offers some hope of basing his thoughts and values on objective **truth**. Likewise, a diary is a means of keeping a permanent record of one's experience in order to provide an independent reference point against the ever-changing stories and lies of Big Brother. Winston's need for a concrete and objective record is symbolised by his attraction to buying the coral paperweight, which in itself bears witness to a previous time:

> It's a little chunk of history that they've forgotten to alter. It's a message from a hundred years ago, if one knew how to read it.

The purpose of a paperweight is to prevent papers from being blown away and lost. This contrasts starkly to Winston's job in the Department of Truth, where he is always destroying documents and photos from the past. Likewise, his memory of nursery rhymes is just fragments. Although apparently trivial in themselves these songs are important because they are historical texts, not the fake products of the Department of Truth: the fake histories and forged photographs, the garbled rewritings of poems now considered offensive, the mechanically composed 'sentimental songs' and poems, and the novels created bureaucratically using a novel-writing machine.

One sign of a good thesis is that it explains quite a lot. Otherwise put, it connects to and casts light upon more than one key theme in the prescribed text. Here the implied argument is that to insist on truth in Oceania is to find oneself considered 'different' and a threat. The discussion following the quote outlines a number of aspects of the novel that are closely connected to this point.

Cuddon's Dictionary of Literary Terms defines symbolism as 'an object ... which represents or "stands for" something else'. My identifying its use is one small example of language analysis in this essay.

12 However, when it comes to Winston and Julia seeking to engage in active **resistance**, to join the Brotherhood, just how limited is Winston's progress toward **truth** becomes apparent: to O'Brien he expresses his willingness to undertake various atrocious acts, such as murdering innocent people, for the cause. Winston has not found an authentic path for himself. He has not developed a considered set of beliefs and values to guide his life. For this reason the first stage in Winston's new path of resistance is to run the risk of acquiring and reading the Goldstein book,

where he finds a 'more powerful, more systematic' (p. 161) and historical case for the coming revolution 'through the spread of enlightenment' (p. 210). This suggests that credible, well-considered texts have the potential to transform our ideas and values, to guide us toward happier and more authentic human experiences. Thus Winston's early impressions of Goldstein's book are that 'it was bliss, it was eternity' (p. 150); it fascinates and reassures him (p. 161).

Above all it is important to know a prescribed text well in order to be able to perceive connections between different parts of the text.

Section 2: Difference and First Nations people

13 A chosen short text illuminates the importance of articulating a clear statement of values and aspirations. The Uluru Statement from the Heart (2017), in strong contrast to the intolerance of difference in Oceania, urges the importance of recognising and **embracing difference** in Australian history and in contemporary society. In particular, it calls for formal recognition of Australia's First Peoples in the Australian Constitution and parliament. In support of this claim it offers a contextualising sketch of the history of our First Peoples, some broad aims and the reasoning behind them, and invites other Australians to join in this cause.

Section 2 of the essay begins with a 'set up' paragraph explaining both the themes to be pursued and how they relate to the discussion in the first part of the essay.

Much of this paragraph consists of a summary: that is, the foundations upon which the argument will build.

2.1 Recognising difference

14 This Statement not only calls for the recognition of difference but, in its approach and use of language, seeks to demonstrate how different cultures can co-exist. This is in strong contrast to the insistence on conformity and homogeneity in *Nineteen Eighty-Four*. It begins by offering historical context, with a brief account of the history of the 'first sovereign Nations of the Australian continent'. The language takes in three perspectives: in addition to First Nations culture, it refers to the broader Australian contexts of 'common law' and 'science'. Thus, from the outset, the statement integrates First Nations and Western perspectives. Similarly it uses a measure that is common in conventional Western thinking—statistics—in noting that 'Proportionally, we are the

most incarcerated people on the planet'. This choice of telling detail adds power and persuasiveness to the argument that a great wrong in this country needs to be addressed: 'the torment of our powerlessness'. Thus, unlike *Nineteen Eighty-Four*, in which both history and context are denied, the statement offers an **objective** and **factual** foundation for its claims. In stark contrast Winston is finally made to accept that 2 + 2 = 5. Indeed he confronts a situation 'more terrifying than torture or death' (p. 31): a world with no objective context. The blatant Party slogan is to 'control the past' (199) in order to also control the future through systematic lying and fakery.

There are many exciting texts to explore that clearly relate well to the themes for which this novel is famous (see commentary after paragraph 1). Here I have taken a different path, in response to the syllabus, in examining some of its themes in the light of another culture. It is essential, however, to ensure you do not go off track. Being able to draw meaningful connections to the prescribed text is a key indicator that the thesis is indeed relevant and useful.

Although I haven't identified 'objective' and 'factual' as keywords, they clearly relate to the keyword 'truth' so I have bolded them here to illustrate continuance of that theme.

2.1.1 Recognising spirituality

15 A key element of First Nations difference addressed in this statement is the emphasis on spiritual values: it is noted that the legalistic term 'sovereignty' has a spiritual nature, based on 'ownership of the soil'. This perspective, stressing the land itself, is in strong contrast to Western practice, in which ownership of the land is expressed in lines drawn on paper and is usually a means of acquiring wealth. In the documentary series *First Australians* (Perkins, 2008) the connection between spirituality and the land is explained in greater detail. The opening sequence of each episode recounts a creation story in which:

> Before the Dreaming all that moved on the land was the wind. Then came life. Giant beings came down from the sky, came from the sea, from within the earth itself. Part-animal, part-human, these beings travelled the land. They danced and made love. They hunted and fought, creating a landscape as they went. In everything they touched they left their essence, their life force, making the land itself sacred to those that would follow them.

This story provides the basis for other parts of the series, in which the sacredness of waterholes, trees, certain locations, geographical features, and so on, is revealed through stories of early contact with white people. In Episode 4 it is explained that for the Arrente desert people of Central Australia, their Dreaming is known through the *Altyerra*, the sacred law that 'leads their life'. Aerial photography of the Caterpillar Ranges, accompanied by a voiceover telling the story of the Caterpillar people who are their ancestors, visually conveys the resemblance of these rock formations to caterpillars. The effect is to bring the landscape alive with meaning through the reader's exposure to this perspective.

Broadly, the organisational principle of this second part of the essay is based on drawing contrasts between Nineteen Eighty-Four and the Uluru Statement. As this statement is quite brief I looked for more substantiating detail in other appropriate sources.

16 The difference in spirituality between the colonising peoples and the First Peoples is made apparent in the story of three German missionaries who came to Arrente land from Adelaide. The narrator records that at first the gifts of flour and sugar were very welcome but they came at the price of having to wear clothes and to listen to the 'endless German sermons'. It also became clear to the elders, who began to shun the missionaries, 'what their game was: that these people didn't respect their beliefs' (Peter Vallee, in Perkins, 2008). The missionaries apparently did not recognise, nor seek to enquire about, the nature of First Nations spiritual beliefs but instead aimed to stamp them out. They also misinterpreted the intent when Arrente men and women dressed up and decorated themselves for their dances, fearing they were about to engage in savage rituals and calling them 'heathens'. This word strongly conveys how perceived difference can be used to put down others. Some meanings of this word are 'irreligious', 'unenlightened' and 'barbarous' (the *Macquarie Dictionary*). Ironically, however, in their creation story the Arrente people already had their equivalent of the book of Genesis, which the missionaries taught them. According to Herman Malbunka, '... the white people wanted to convert them, to change them. They wouldn't change because of what they had learnt. We have our *Twerrenge*'. Similarly to Winston's experience in *Nineteen Eighty-Four*, the individual is resistant to pressures to conform: our difference is an intrinsic part of human experience.

The paragraph above offers another example of getting down to concrete detail within the discussion (see Chapter 4, 'Quoting', for more on this). The last sentence draws a clear connection to the prescribed text.

Taking a close look at the meaning of a keyword is one way of examining language and its use.

17 The Uluru theme that different cultures can co-exist in mutual respect is reinforced by the story of one of the first Indigenous 'converts', Tjallkabotta, who according to Max Stuart came to be an *Ngkarte*, a 'church leader', both for the Christian church, where he became an evangelist, and for his native kin. In reality, he did not 'convert' (change completely) to Christianity, but adopted an additional system of knowledge, for 'He knew every *Tywerrenge* and never let on' (Max Stuart). By using Indigenous words and concepts, the documentary offers to non-Indigenous viewers the opportunity of likewise adding to their cultural knowledge. *Tywerrenge* are sacred objects, such as stones or wooden tablets, often with totemic markings that convey aspects of the *Altyerra*. According to Stuart, Tjallkabotta was a 'visionary', one who indeed learnt to, in the words of the Uluru Statement, 'walk in two worlds' at once, combining the worlds of the Christian 'god in the sky' and also the law in the land. One marker of his ability to bridge this divide of difference is in his adopting the name 'Moses'. This draws a connection between the biblical figure who was given his people's law in the tablets with the Ten Commandments, and the native practice of inscribing *Altyerra* on sacred objects. Tjallkabotta understood his native land and culture through its customs and language but was also comfortable living among Europeans and understanding their world, sharing their language and thought.

Although I am not specifically talking about the use of literary devices in this paragraph, the discussion about the meaning of 'conversion' and about the name 'Moses' responds to the syllabus aim of examining how texts represent human experiences through close attention to language. The significance of using Indigenous language in the documentary series (Perkins, 2008) is explained in the paragraph itself.

18 The Uluru Statement's insistence on the spiritual dimension of 'sovereignty' illustrates the importance of articulating one's values and beliefs. In *Nineteen Eighty-Four* even objective common sense is considered 'the heresy of heresies' (68). *Heresy* is a term generally used in relation to religious thought but in Oceania, any kind of spiritual principle is denied and the Party defines any unapproved thinking as 'heresy'. This explains the significance of the nursery rhyme 'Oranges and Lemons', which tells what various church bells 'say'. This rhyme dates back to a time when the church had been a living institution, when the bells were rung for a purpose and had meaning. Winston, who has no

memory of hearing church bells ring, is dimly aware that there are deeper dimensions to life than the Party pretends.

19 However, the Party, in seeking to eliminate any possibility of heresy, avoids the historical mistake made by states and churches in the past: that is, of making martyrs out of dissenters. O'Brien explains that the example of such martyrs could encourage others. Rather, O'Brien seeks to make minds 'perfect', defined as eliminating all **resistance** and difference: a complete 'conversion' by torture and brainwashing. As he warns Winston:

> Everything will be dead inside you. Never again will you be capable of love, or friendship, or joy of living, or laughter, or curiosity, or courage, or integrity. You will be hollow. We shall squeeze you empty, and then we shall fill you with ourselves. (p. 206)

Note: A section on exploring and affirming difference has been deleted from this essay for reasons of space and simplicity. This section corresponded and contrasted to Section 1.2 on the suppression of difference in Nineteen Eighty-Four.

2.2 Mounting resistance to oppression

20 While the private **resistance** of Winston and Julia is ultimately futile, another contrasting theme in the Uluru Statement is its call for positive change, to celebrate difference and bridge the divide between the First Nations and the broader community. In contrast to the emphasis in *Nineteen Eighty-Four* on intolerance of all deviation from official values, the Uluru Statement promotes not merely tolerance but appreciation of the potential of difference. The language balances the formal register of 'substantive constitutional change and structural reform' with the more poetic expression of allowing 'this ancient sovereignty [to] shine through as a fuller expression of Australia's nationhood'. Here, the figurative expression 'shine through' metonymically implies sunlight and relief from a present state of darkness. This delicately evokes the **truth** of a negative past while putting the emphasis on a positive future.

A metonym is 'a figure of speech in which the name of an attribute or a thing is substituted for the thing itself' (Dictionary of Literary Terms and Literary Theory, 1992). In this case, the attribute of 'light' is taken to represent the sun.

'Register' is defined in the glossary of the English Standard syllabus as 'The degree of formality or informality of language used for a particular purpose or in a particular social setting'.

2.2.1 Reaching out to all Australians

21 The language also attempts to bridge the difference divide in other ways by reaching out directly to all Australians: 'We invite you to walk with us in a movement of the Australian people for a better future'. Characterising this as an Australian rather than First Nations movement rhetorically emphasises the need for unity and dialogue. Similarly in the first sentence, rather than listing the different states and regions from which conference delegates came, it refers to what unites them by referring to their 'coming from all points of the southern sky'. This figurative language is a further reminder of First Nations connections to nature, again metonymically conveyed by the 'southern sky', and also evokes the creation story of giants coming from the sky. Likewise, in speaking to a future where 'our children … will walk in two worlds and their culture will be a gift to our country' it insists both on the continuance and viability of First Nations culture and its coexistence with the wider community.

I could also have discussed strategies of rhetoric here. This term is addressed in the commentary on the 'by numbers' essay in Chapter 6.

Conclusion

22 The grim, inhuman world of *Nineteen Eighty-Four* illustrates that difference is at the heart of human experiences, and demonstrates the importance of expressing and exploring our difference, by showing the consequences when others try to **suppress** it. Difference is inherent to human experiences, in individual values, thoughts, feelings and desires, and in collective forms such as culture and language. It has been shown that suppression of difference adversely affects those it touches.

In the conclusion various strands of my thesis and argument are tied together. This goes beyond merely restating the argument from the introduction (the thesis statement is restated here, in part) and summarising subsequent discussion, to draw out some further implications: it focuses on discussing difference as a key part of human experience, as covered in the body of the essay. The organisational principle used in this conclusion is to summarise first the prescribed text and then the supplementary text.

23 In contrast the Uluru Statement, based on a response to the **truth** of Australian history, offers a very different perspective: recognising, exploring and **embracing difference** and seeking to bridge cultures through mutual understanding. It leads by example, employing the

formal language of mainstream politics and legislation while incorporating First Nations cultural values, such as ties to nature and family, and connection to land and language. In a direct address to the reader (via the use of the second person) it continues the metaphor of a journey and a dialogue: 'We invite you to walk with us in a movement of the Australian people'. The word 'movement' is a pun, as it refers both to the furtherance of this cause as a movement and to the 'movement' of peoples across the native land in a metaphorical 'trek across this vast country'. Rather than using the imperative form, in saying just 'Walk with us', which would sound like a command, instead it extends an invitation to all Australians ('We invite you') to do so, to engage with and understand the culture of the traditional custodians of the land. Thus it models how difference can be affirmed and celebrated to create new, better outcomes for that 'fuller expression of Australia's nationhood' in which today's young become 'our hope for the future'. In complete contrast to the hateful persecution of difference in *Nineteen Eighty-Four*, the Uluru Statement suggests that embracing difference can help create a happier society that innovates and flourishes, and which draws on the creative possibilities of human diversity and difference. It stresses what unites us, like the southern sky and the land in which we all live, but which many of us could better appreciate and understand.

My reference to the 'imperative' case is one example of examining language in terms of grammar (as specified in the English Standard syllabus), in order to better understand how texts shape meaning. The imperative is the 'verb mood specialised for use in command, requests, and the like ....' (the Macquarie Dictionary).

EXERCISES

1. Look at old HSC papers and find questions on texts you are studying: NESA has a range of former papers and specimen papers available online. Sketch out a rough plan for an essay to answer it. Before starting, note whether the question is 'open' or 'closed'.
2. Write a thesis essay for the most recent English text you've read.
3. Do one for each English text you have studied so far.

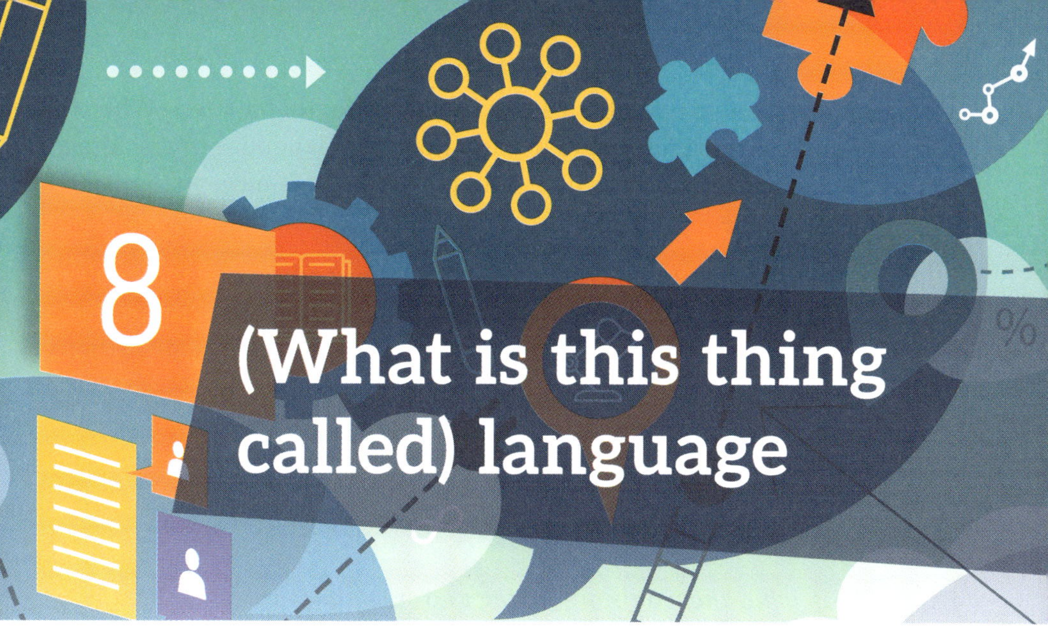

8 (What is this thing called) language

Language, language, language

In HSC English, your essays are marked not merely on your knowledge and ideas, but also on your ability to use language to express yourself. As you draft and redraft essays, the work you put in to polish word choice and expression will pay off doubly, as your thoughts become clearer and more precise, and your better use of language creates a favourable impression.

There's another strong reason why you need to become more aware of language: language itself is a central part of the syllabus. The syllabus requires that you respond to and compose different types of language usage in different *genres* (kinds of writing), write in different styles, at different *registers* (levels) of formality (from formal essay English to other registers), and across a variety of forms. Becoming more aware of language also gives you extra 'ammunition' and support for your argument. For example, in the sample essay in Chapter 6 I looked at specialised meanings of words and at the various ways in which particular effects were achieved. This can be helpful in examining poetry, which often uses dense forms of expression. In this essay and in the sample thesis essay (Chapter 7) I also analysed the use of language for persuasive purposes. Each form, such as drama, film and multimedia, has its own language, and so do different genres.

Of course we all know what language is … we use it all the time. You're using it right now as you read. It seems as automatic as breathing the air. And yet, how much do we actually know about language? (How much does the average person really know about air, or breathing for that matter?) When it comes to questions asking you to discuss the use of language in a reading passage, or as part of an essay question, many students have virtually no idea what is expected.

When asked to comment on language, students often just look for similes and metaphors, and perhaps imagery. These forms are called 'figurative' language, and yes, they are *examples* of language usage, but language is far more than that.

What is 'language'?

Language is *what the words are saying* and *how they express it.* That is a definition worth committing to memory, because it explains that language can be virtually any aspect of a text. When you examine language, you should start by examining the meanings it represents, secondly looking at the ways it works. Language is not just 'words' and literary devices, but their meaning, their effect. Without considering the meaning conveyed by words, language is—well—meaningless! 'Language' is also the structure of a text, the genre in which it is written, the conventions and codes it uses, and any means of communicating a message, which may include very subtle ways.

LANGUAGE IS:

1. **words**
2. **what they mean**
3. **the effect they have**
4. **how they are used to get the meaning across.**

Language of viewing and representation

The English syllabus considers multimedia, films, paintings and photographs as 'texts'. The language they use goes beyond words, and can draw on whole other systems, codes and conventions to convey meaning. An introductory list would include the following:

Non-verbal communication (for various media):

- body language
- tone of voice

- facial expressions
- gesture
- dress

Painting/Other artworks:

- perspective
- colours
- brushstroke
- foregrounding
- juxtaposition
- collage
- balance of elements

Film language:

- composition of the frame
- different kinds of camera shots—close-up, medium close-up, etc., tracking shots, dolly shots
- editing
- transitions between scenes—fades, wipes, dissolves, etc.
- montage (editing technique of juxtaposing a series of images to make meaning)
- framing—what's in the frame, and what is not

Multimedia:

- sound
- hyperlinks
- menu
- film and other graphical material

Word choice

Professional writers, especially creative writers, use words very carefully. It was Samuel Taylor Coleridge who advised looking at a piece of writing and asking how would the meaning be altered if one word (or several) were changed. Ask yourself how an idea could have been expressed differently. What effect would this have had? Why did the writer employ this precise choice of words?

Reading and language (read read read, write write write)

In a radio interview broadcast not long before his death, Australia's Nobel prizewinning author Patrick White was asked what advice he would give to budding writers:

'Read read read. Write write write' was his reply. The more you read, not only is your store of knowledge enriched, but your familiarity with language is enhanced. Reading and writing are two sides of the one coin. Quite apart from whatever else you learn, you are learning about language every time you read.

Of course the more knowledge you have, the better support you'll be able to give to your arguments in all subjects. In English you will engage with a variety of texts that offer varying information and perspectives on any given subject. These may include:

- clippings from newspapers and magazines
- internet sites
- promotional or informational brochures from various organisations
- TV or radio broadcasts
- non-fiction books on a study area
- critical writings—collections or single articles on an author or work
- film, radio or stage adaptations.

Critics and commentaries

Year 12 students are not expected to become 'critics' themselves but you may find it very helpful to look at some critical writings, commentaries or study guides on a work or author. Any of these resources can provide helpful background information and fresh insights. In general, don't forget to criticise the critics too. This doesn't mean to 'knock' them, but to be aware of possible defects in their arguments.

Some language terms

In terms of 'proving' a thesis or other argument, some of the best evidence you can provide in an English essay is discussion of language. You don't just quote a passage but you must also examine details, explaining what you think it *means* and *how* words are used to express this.

Your notes on each text should include samples of language and discussion of its effects. I have provided a list of helpful language terms below. Familiarising yourself with them will expand your repertoire of language discussion skills—and help you become more aware of your own usage!

Antithesis	Use of contrasting terms in conjunction.
Contrast	Directly comparing different matters to highlight differences.
Devices	Any means used by the writer to achieve a particular effect, such as: • suspense • drama • plot • jokes • incongruity (things being 'out of place').
Genre	The type of writing used or the particular activity for which it is used. Priests use language differently to police, a recipe uses language differently to a fan letter, a birthday greeting is different to an obituary. Literary genres include westerns, science fiction, romance, thrillers, and so on. It's important to realise that the purpose for which language is used will directly affect the use of language. A romance novel is unlikely to use heavy philosophical concepts, nor will it use the pseudo-scientific jargon of 'Sci Fi'. Each genre has its own conventions, which help to distinguish it from others.
Onomatopoeia	The sound of the word imitates the sound to which it refers, such as 'splash', 'beep', etc.
Oxymoron	A contradiction in terms; for example, 'honest criminal'.
Paradox	An apparent contradiction. In William Blake's 'The Sick Rose', the rose, often used as a symbol of love, is itself afflicted by the 'dark secret love' of an invisible worm that will destroy it.

Parallelism	The sustained drawing out of two similar stories or characters with common elements; for example, the theme of fidelity in Mozart's *Così Fan Tutte* is paralleled by the same theme in the lives of Lewis, Henry and others, in *Così*.
Point of view	The standpoint from which the piece is written. Who is telling the story? Is the narrator speaking in the first or third person? From whose point (or points) of view is *Stasiland* written? *Romulus, My Father?* The films *A Beautiful Mind* and *Life of Pi*? Does the narrator know all, or is their knowledge limited? Is the standpoint historical or contemporary?
Pun	A play on words. Puns are often based on words that sound similar or that have similar meanings. 'Many are cold but few are frozen' puns on a well-known saying. 'Life depends on the liver' has two quite separate meanings, both of which may be intended at the same time.
Purpose	What is the writer attempting to convey, and to whom? For example: **didactic** works are intended to teach; propaganda aims to persuade for political purposes. Other purposes are: to be frivolous, entertaining, amusing, informative. And so on!
Register	The 'level' of language used. An academic or a diplomat uses a high, formal register. An essay uses formal language, not slang. Some journalists use very simple language, others employ a higher register.
Rhythm	Does the language have a particular rhythm or does it use a particular form, such as blank verse, a limerick, a sonnet, etc.?
Style	How the language is 'dressed'. Styles can be simple or complex, wordy or concise, 'mannered' or direct, flowing or staccato ('jerky').
Tone	The writer's *attitude* to the subject matter (a very important consideration, which you will often be asked to comment upon). Examples: humorous, ironic (extremely common, but tricky), sarcastic, didactic, playful, mocking, emotional, angry, loving, eulogistic, morbid, conversational, absurd, quirky, zany.
Vocabulary	The reservoir of words from which we choose. Vocabulary is an immensely helpful asset in language. You can never know too many words. Some people certainly have richer vocabularies than others, but the good news is that these riches come absolutely free! There are times when one word will sum up so much: Look up the word *altruistic* if you don't know it already.

Vocabulary (cont.)	It's defined in the *Macquarie Dictionary* as 'the principle or practice of seeking the welfare of others'. In other words, an altruist is an unselfish person motivated to look after people. It takes many words to explain the idea though, doesn't it! The word 'unselfish' doesn't quite express the same meaning, or in as much detail. To learn a new word is often to learn a new concept as well! The renowned French novelist Marcel Proust valued words so highly that he devised an extreme way of learning new ones. He'd write them on strips of paper and hang them with pegs on a clothes line in his room. Why not try bluetacking new words all over the house, on your bedroom mirror ... see how long it takes to infuriate your parents or flatmates! (For enthusiasts only, but you probably wouldn't be the first student to do it!)
Word choice	The bigger your vocabulary, the richer are your opportunities for word use. When analysing a writer's use of language, consider why one word was used in preference to another. What other words could have been used, and how would this have affected the meaning?

Figures of speech

Figurative language is language that is not literal (that is, not intended to be 'taken for real'), but is used for effect. Such language is heavily used by poets but is also common elsewhere.

Metaphor	An important and extremely common figure of speech, it is where 'one thing is described in terms of another'. Paul writes in *The Stolen Children* that 'my shadow was my best friend'. This powerful metaphor expresses his lonely and empty life. This figure of speech is so important that I've taken it out of alphabetical order to put it at the top of the list!
Hyperbole	A gross exaggeration: 'Millions of people came to the end-of-school-year party last night'.
Imagery	We normally refer to imagery as 'painting a picture with words' but actually it can appeal to any of the five senses. Poet Bruce Dawe uses much imagery in the garden of '*Homo Suburbiensis*': 'the hoarse rasping tendrils of pumpkin flourish clumsy whips and their foliage sprawls ...'

Irony	Saying something other than what you intend people to understand. We could mean the opposite ('lovely day' during a storm), or we could be using *understatement*. For example, 'I didn't try too hard' might mean 'I didn't try at all'.
Metonymy	A detail is used to represent the whole; for example, 'I saw three sails on the horizon' means 'ships', not sails.
Simile	Like metaphors, similes are a comparison, but they use 'like' or 'as'. Metaphors are a comparison where we say that one item *is* another. For example: *Simile*: 'This film is like a roller-coaster ride.' *Metaphor*: 'This film is a roller-coaster ride.'

What different *effects* do these two versions have on you, the reader?

Some further language vocabulary

effect
evoke
atmosphere
compare
structure
anticlimax
sequence
feelings
connotation
denotation
objective
subjective
theme
issue

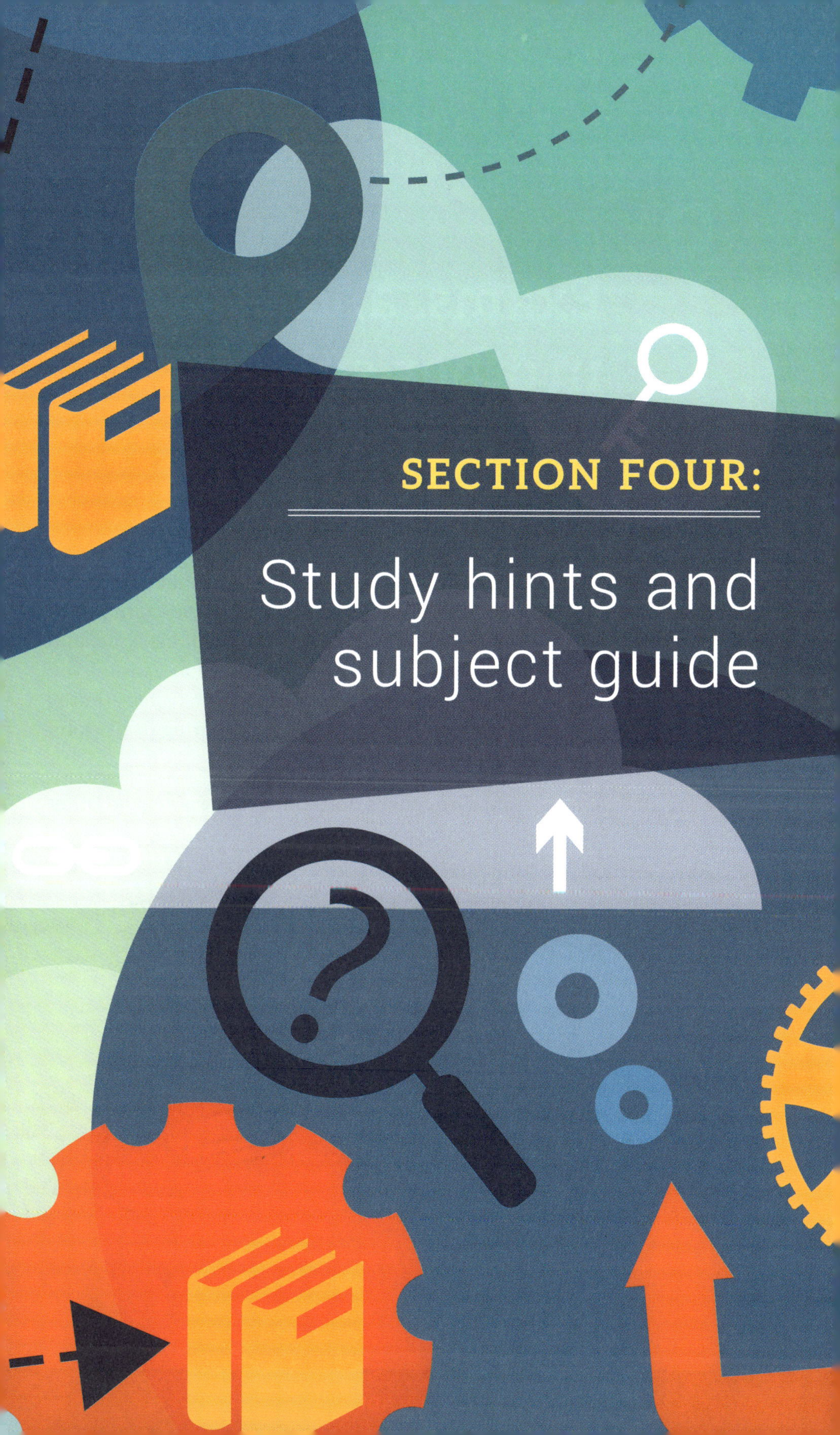

SECTION FOUR:

Study hints and subject guide

9 Exams, and essays in other subjects

So: if a good essay takes several drafts, how can you be expected to write an 'extended response' in 40 minutes and one draft only, in the exam room? Good question. Firstly, don't panic: examiners are aware of this issue, and take it into account. Secondly, everyone's in the same position. Thirdly, you can prepare yourself for exams by 'rehearsing' with old exam papers, timing yourself and working under exam-like conditions, by writing draft exam essays and by organising your study well.

There are several important differences between exam essays and other essays:

- There is a strict time limit (and, although you are not marked according to the length of your essay, a detailed, complete essay does impress).
- You don't have time to polish a rough draft.
- You can't research. (That is why your study must be as well organised as possible beforehand.)
- Planning is essential because there is no time to change your argument midway through the essay.

Exam strategies

- Read the entire paper quickly. Start to think about which questions you'll do, and how to answer them.
- Try outlining a quick essay plan for each question before you start to answer any. Sometimes, forgotten information or 'inspiration' will come to your aid when you return to that question. It's as if the unconscious mind works on automatic pilot!
- If you get stuck with one essay, go on to the others before coming back to it.
- Make sure you read ALL instructions and follow them exactly (it's easy to overlook something important).
- Know in advance how much time is allowed for each question, and stick to it. It may be tempting to write extra material on one question, but the gains you could make will be minimal compared to the marks you might lose in the next question.
- Some questions are split into a number of different parts, each with a separate weighting of marks. Look at what each question is worth and tailor the length of your response and the amount of time you spend on it, accordingly. If a question is worth twelve marks, and part (a) is worth three marks, you should spend about a quarter of the total time allocated to that question on part (a).
- Make doubly sure that you answer ALL parts of the question. If the question makes two or more demands, answer all of them.
- Try to leave a minute or so to check back over each essay, fixing up any glaring omissions or errors.

A sample exam essay

Following is an example of an exam essay. As noted in Chapter 7, the virtue of the thesis essay as a study tool is that it helps you organise your thoughts and your supporting data to the point that they are pre-digested. It is excellent preparation for exams and offers practice in developing an argument that mounts a clear thesis uniting the discussion, analysis, selection and treatment of texts.

This exam essay was developed in response to a previous HSC English Area of Study—Belonging—but the same principles and approach would apply to writing an exam essay on the present Common module: Texts and Human Experiences.

You might also note that this essay employs a different organisational principle to the thesis essay: here the argument is developed text by text rather than theme by theme.

'If you are alone you belong entirely to yourself. If you are accompanied by even one companion you belong only half to yourself, or even less, in proportion to the thoughtlessness of his conduct; and if you have more than one companion you will fall more deeply into the same plight.' (Leonardo da Vinci) To what extent do the texts you have studied support this understanding of belonging? In your response, refer to your prescribed text, and at least TWO other related texts of your own choosing.

1 Da Vinci's understanding of belonging is that it diminishes our individualism and integrity. We become less ourselves, due to the influence of others' behaviour, attitudes and expectations. This is supported to some extent in the texts I have studied, but mainly when characters are incompatible. Study of Charles Dickens' *Great Expectations,* the film *Australian Rules* and Judith Wright's poem 'The Company of Lovers' suggests, however, that belonging can help us to reach our potential and thus truly become ourselves. We can belong to others without jeopardising our individuality and our own principles, despite various obstacles.

2 In *Great Expectations,* belonging can come at the cost of being oneself. As a boy, Pip finds it difficult to express himself in the family home. When guests are present, he is insulted and told to keep quiet. Dickens uses metaphor to suggest that the conversation, pretending to be for his betterment, in reality tortures Pip like a dumb animal: he 'might have been an unfortunate little bull' who is 'touched up by these moral goads'. When he encounters the worse than 'thoughtless' influence of Magwitch, Pip is led to steal from his own sister and to tell lies as well, behaviour he knows to be unacceptable: again, the company he keeps lessens him.

3 Equally, belonging to a 'gentlemanly' class does not agree well with Pip: the Finches of the Grove club is foolish, drunken and quarrelsome, and members like Bentley Drummle are odious. Dickens uses contrasting

language to demonstrate the reality starkly: Pip and Herbert spend 'as much money' as they can to get as little back as possible, while racking up dangerous debt. Pip notes that the 'gay fiction' of happiness is contradicted by the 'bare skeleton' of truth that they are miserable. The 'torture' exacted by Estella on his visits further illustrates Da Vinci's 'plight' of belonging.

4 However, not to belong to others creates the plight of withering away. Dickens conveys through imagery that Miss Havisham's life, shut off from others, is unnatural and cold: she is initially described by Pip as yellow, faded, a 'waxwork'. She lives behind dark walls inside the decaying Satis House, 'in which her life was hidden from the sun'. The sun symbolises human love: without it, we wither like plants, rather than blooming. Estella too is taught by Havisham that daylight is her 'enemy and destroyer' and she has grown up loveless and cold. She knits away mechanically when Pip declares his love for her. The simile of her knitting fingers being like a 'dumb alphabet' conveys that she is emotionally stunted.

5 Estella's tragedy is a combination of two disasters: first, in accord with Da Vinci's theme, her life has been shaped by thoughtless others like Miss Havisham, who used her to take revenge on men. When she does finally marry, it is another unsuitable match, to the 'brute' Drummle, and she ends up alone, having wasted her life and her fortune. Secondly, like Havisham she is isolated from the sun of human love. By the end of the novel, belonging to herself is no great consolation. Dickens uses stilted formal language to convey her emotions, demonstrating that she still puts up verbal walls against others: she speaks of her 'wifely duty' not being 'incompatible with the admission of that remembrance' of the importance of her friendship with Pip.

6 Thus the study of *Great Expectations* suggests that, in contrast to Da Vinci's view, belonging to others is key to becoming ourself. However, belonging with the wrong people can diminish us. Pip grows into a better person when he makes decisions about whom he should associate with, and how he should interact with them. He stops exerting bad influence on Herbert and instead helps to set up his business. He shows compassion and care for Magwitch, and eventually comes to realise how important humble Joe and Biddy are to him.

7 That we need others in order to achieve our potential is underlined clearly in *Australian Rules*, where the 'great expectations' of winning the Aussie Rules grand final are shared by the whole community. This is

emphasised from the opening frames of the film, with a close-up on dry, cracked earth symbolising the 'common ground' and common interests of the white and the Aboriginal communities. The voiceover by the central character Blackie is used to draw this to our attention, stating that Prospect Bay, which he describes as 'bloody hopeless', would not be in the grand final without the Aboriginal players: in fact, 'we wouldn't even have a team'. The team's colours, black and white, featured throughout the movie, symbolise this need for unity. In contrast to Da Vinci's theme, this movie suggests it is important to belong and to contribute to the community.

8 In fact, it is the contributions of very individual people to the team that make it so strong, despite the town's divisive attitudes of racism, sexism and anti-intellectualism. Two people who make decisive contributions to the grand final win are the Aboriginal player Dumby and Blackie's mother, who works out the winning strategy. Blackie uses language very well, unlike 'Arks' ('ask') the coach and Blackie's Dad, locks himself in the toilet to read the dictionary, is called 'a gutless bloody wonder', a 'pussy' and is accused of 'wanking'. The stark contrast of language register demonstrates the thoughtlessness of Blackie's company, but ultimately Blackie triumphs and wins the final play of the game by being himself, and playing against the coach's instructions.

9 When division and intolerance take over again, after the game is won, Blackie can no longer belong, without damage to his integrity. He feels forced to leave Prospect Bay because of intolerance. In a climactic scene where he is surprised together with his Aboriginal girlfriend Clarence, he is assaulted by his father, who forces him to deny Clarence in front of her. He is diminished by this, and does not belong to himself at this point, so that he has little choice but to regain his freedom and integrity by leaving.

10 Similarly to *Great Expectations* then, belonging to the wrong circles, and barriers to belonging, are much bigger problems than the influence of belonging. So long as the community stays committed to thoughtless attitudes, Prospect Bay will remain deep in its plight. The footy legend Glen Bright quotes that 'When men (sic) get together wonderful things happen'. When, however, people are divided, dreadful things happen, people fail to grow, and the town reverts to being 'bloody hopeless'.

11 Judith Wright's poem 'The Company of Lovers' expresses almost the opposite viewpoint to Da Vinci's: belonging is more important than individualism and integrity: 'We meet and part now over all the world'.

The repeated use of the first person plural 'we' invites us to feel part of this company. Through the use of the internal half-rhyme 'meet/part' she suggests the equivalence of these two verbs, and conveys that belonging is only a 'brief happiness' and therefore precious. In contrast to *Australian Rules* and to *Great Expectations*, expectations and other pursuits become just the 'many things' that we 'throw away' in favour of the sheer desire for intimate company.

12 The use of very general terms like 'company' and 'over all the world' to describe the comfort of belonging is in stark contrast to Wright's precise description of being alone. 'Belonging to ourself' merely diminishes us: it means just to live with a 'chilling heart', to live with 'my fear'. Our ultimate destiny is to belong only to ourselves in the 'narrow grave', in which 'we shall be lonely' and thus belonging to oneself is a form of death, a theme underlined by Wright's sparing but telling use of adjectives: 'lost', 'brief', 'chilling', 'dark'.

13 Da Vinci's description of belonging is partly supported by these texts. Belonging can diminish us, leading us to behave in ways contrary to our own beliefs, but it also provides opportunities to grow and to better ourselves; as the lives of Miss Havisham and Estella demonstrate, to be shut off from other people is to wither. However, Pip and Blackie learn that it is important to make good choices in whom we associate with, and in how we relate to others. We can learn to belong better, as a pathway to happiness and to achieving our own potential: only when we reach our potential do we truly belong to ourselves.

Exam hints: Standard English Papers

As one example of meeting exam requirements, here are some hints for treating the Standard English papers.

The format of exam papers in all subjects can vary over the years so your best guide is always the instructions in the exam paper itself, which you must always read carefully. This principle applies to all instructions in the paper: both any general instructions at the start of the paper and instructions specific to each question. Take particular care with time management in accord with the stated guidelines as to how much time to spend on each question, and take a moment to read any marking guidelines that are stated.

Don't assume that it is adequate to just give a good answer in a few words. Assume that the examiners will be unconvinced until you demonstrate your comprehension fully using the three-step method (see Chapter 4). The more marks the question is worth, the more your answer needs to be complete and satisfying.

Other hints

- Read or examine all the texts and all the questions before answering. Try to determine the overall *tone*—the author's attitude to the subject matter—and the theme or opinion being developed.
- Take careful note of the mark allocation per question; these vary considerably.
- Answer questions with reference to the *context* of the text(s). Often the context of a phrase or detail will indicate a different meaning from dictionary or everyday meanings.
- Make sure your answer is from the *text(s)* rather than from your general knowledge!
- Pass over and return to the 'too hard' questions: they may 'click into place' once you've progressed further and relaxed a bit more.
- You may find it helpful to mark relevant passages on the exam paper, to make it easier to find answers.

Composing texts

In Standard English Paper 2 you are likely to be asked to compose a piece of your own. In addition to studying language in its many forms, you are expected to read widely. Knowledge of a wide variety of forms of writing (genres) will help greatly, enriching your general knowledge, your vocabulary and your understanding of the different features of different genres. For specific tasks, expect the unexpected!

Always write with a clear purpose. This will help you stand out from those writers who just pour out ideas haphazardly. The instructions will indicate what is required.

You can practise for this section by writing pieces that vary the use of register, purpose, form, format, audience, role and vocabulary. You might be asked to write a letter, an interview, a play script or some other piece, or to produce a piece for a specific magazine and suggest accompanying graphics. Whatever the task, suit the language and structure to the genre of writing.

You can practise your command of *register* by writing dialogue for two different characters requiring different kinds of speech: for example, compare a politician's public speech with their normal speech at home, or compare 'street-kid' speech with a businessperson's on the same subject.

Examples of different genres

thriller novels	comedy sketches	political speeches
autobiographies	press releases	obituaries
TV news broadcasts	encyclopaedia entries	hypertext writing
recipes	government reports	advertisements
diaries	'blogs' (web logs)	love letters
feature articles	drama scripts	hypertext novels
song lyrics	eulogies	editorials
film reviews	fan letters	raps

Essay writing in other subjects

While this book focuses on the essay or extended response in English, all the skills you practise will aid your writing in short responses, in other genres (such as reports) and in other HSC subjects also. Contrary to what many people imagine, the English essay makes as many demands as any other kind, as the specified outcomes in the syllabus make explicit. The best English essays are analytical and critical, detailed and specific; they interpret and explain relevant facts and ideas. In fact, English is especially demanding since it emphasises not only your knowledge of the topic, but also your ability to formulate an individual response and to use language well.

However, don't assume that expectations are identical in each HSC subject, since the essay can take different forms and operate under different rules. Pay careful attention to your teacher's stipulations and don't hesitate to ask questions if you are still unsure. (Some subjects allow you to include headings and graphs, for example.) Once you have mastered the techniques in this book, you will have little trouble in customising your writing to somewhat different expectations.

Assessment in each subject is focused on the specified outcomes. In many, the emphasis is on your knowledge and understanding of the subject, your ability to explain and discuss issues and topics in relation to appropriate theories, concepts, practices and systems of thought (e.g. the law), rather than on your opinion or individual response.

Extended-response questions may be in the form of a structured response, which requires you to answer a series of questions in order. The individual parts of these questions may each attract separate marks, the final question often being worth the greatest number of marks.

A number of students have successfully adapted the 'thesis essay' idea to other subjects: Economics, Ancient and Modern History, Legal Studies, etc. If you prepare for such exams in this way, bear in mind that the examiner is more interested in your knowledge and understanding than in your personal response, and don't try to simply regurgitate a prepared essay!

Non-argument essay modes

We have seen that the basis of essays in HSC English is the argument, around which the essay is structured. However, argument is only one of four writing modes. Essays and other formal writings commonly use the other three modes too: description, exposition (explanation) and narration. In other subjects, depending on the question, you might use one or more of these modes. It is not uncommon for an essay to use all four modes, in different sections.

Two of these modes can be prescribed in essay questions, where you may be required to 'describe' or 'explain' in some detail. Generally you should still consider using the standard essay structure. Other commonly prescribed 'doing words' are 'evaluate', 'analyse', 'assess' and 'discuss'. Often it is necessary to describe, explain or narrate in order to communicate your knowledge and understanding, before proceeding to evaluate, analyse, assess or discuss.

Familiarising yourself with the meaning of these 'doing words' will help you meet the expectations of your writing. A selection of these can be found at the end of this chapter.

The verbs *describe, explain* and *narrate* are not defined in the 2019 Standard English syllabus, so in the following three sections I use definitions from the *Macquarie Dictionary* and examples drawn from the former BOSTES NSW for the purpose of giving a deeper understanding of non-argument-based writing modes.

Description

The instruction word *describe* is defined in the *Macquarie Dictionary* as 'give an acount of'. Bear in mind that this describing should be relevant to the question.

> Describe important aspects of chemical usage that need to be considered to provide safeguards to the farm environment.
>
> Adapted from 2001 HSC Specimen Paper, Agriculture, NESA

One could write an essay in response to this question, establishing a theme or argument, then in the body *describing* 'important aspects'. Here is a sample essay outline:

Introduction

Chemicals have many positive uses and can be indispensable to many farmers.

If not used correctly, they can have implications for:

1 occupational health and safety of farm workers
2 farm environment generally
3 contaminating produce, and hurting sales and profitability.

So various practices and precautions need to be followed.

Body

1 *Describe* the benefits of chemical usage.
2 *Describe* the positive aspects of chemical usage.
3 Dangers:
  (a) Occupational health and safety—*describe* how chemical usage affects it.
  (b) Farm environment—*describe* chemical usage's possible effects.
4 *Describe* the results of carelessness or abuse of chemical usage.

Conclusion

Briefly restate the theme based on discussion.

Cap off: Chemicals are very useful but can endanger the farm environment.

The key is their proper usage and disposal.

In such an essay you would use the mode of *description* for much of the essay, but still use the usual essay format, basing it on a theme.

Although the following question does not ask you to *describe*, description is implied:

> Evaluate traditional and contemporary approaches to the management and protection of one ecosystem you have studied and one ecosystem evident in the Stimulus Booklet.
>
> Source: 2001 HSC Specimen Paper, Economics, BOSTES NSW

Before *evaluating*, you need to *describe* different approaches to the management and protection of two separate ecosystems.

Exposition (explaining)

To explain is to 'make plain or clear' or to 'make known in detail' (the *Macquarie Dictionary*).

> Explain how an individual economy (other than Australia) is endeavouring to promote its level of economic development, in an environment where globalisation is affecting living standards.
>
> Source: 2001 HSC Specimen Paper, Economics, BOSTES NSW

In the above essay, much of the body would be devoted to *explaining* an economy's efforts to promote its economic development, and perhaps *describing* the environment of globalisation and its effects on living standards.

The following is a possible essay outline (based on a fictional economy).

Introduction

The economy of Troglia is attempting to promote its economic development in the following ways:

- economic reform program suggested by World Bank
- taking advantage of freed-up trade opportunities
- attracting investment capital for target industries
- promoting tourism.

Body

- *Explain* the benefits of economic reform for economic development.
- *Explain* how freer trade can aid economic development.
- *Explain* the role of target industries in promoting economic development.
- *Explain* the value of tourism for economic development.

Conclusion

Globalisation offers challenges and benefits to Troglia. Troglia is responding so as to maximise its opportunities for economic development.

Narration

Like 'argument', narration is a mode that is unlikely to be specified in the 'doing words' of an essay question. However, at times it is helpful to 'tell a story': to give historical background to an event or phenomenon, to explain the sequence of events, or to narrate how you conducted primary research.

Suggestions for other subjects

The following are some general suggestions to help you come to grips with the particular requirements of essays in subjects other than English:

- You are marked not merely on your knowledge and on your ability to present that knowledge in a well-structured, sustained way, but specifically on the designated outcomes for each unit of study you take. Become familiar with these outcomes and with any marking guidelines stated. Criteria might include: wide range of sources, using up-to-date sources, ability to make use of the stimulus text, and understanding of key concepts.
- It is especially important to *shape* and *structure* your response according to the question and target outcomes, not to get bogged down in mere data for the sake of it.
- Pay close attention to the 'doing words' in the question.
- Consult specialised study guides for that subject.
- Read past examination papers and the specimen papers available on the NESA website.
- Study actively, always thinking about themes and issues. Ask questions as you study. Interpret information: What significance do these statistics have? What are the implications? How do they affect my ideas about this topic? Does this source agree with other sources or contradict them?
- Practise on previous exam papers in that subject, under exam conditions.
- Go over all your returned assessments: What are your strengths and weaknesses, and how can you improve both? Ask your teacher for additional feedback if necessary.

- For assignments, keep within specified word limits unless your teacher states otherwise. (Ten per cent allowance either way is often acceptable.)

Structured-response exam questions

An example of a structured-response question is the following:

> Question 9—Heritage and Identity (30 marks)
>
> (a) Using the source above and your own knowledge, answer the following:
>
> (i) Explain how indigenous art has been exploited for commercial gain.
>
> (ii) What does the NIAAA spokesman mean in his last sentence as it relates to Aboriginal art?
>
> (b) To what extent have contemporary expressions of Aboriginal heritage and identity contributed to the strengthening of Aboriginal culture? Use your Local Aboriginal Community Case Study in your answer.
>
> Source: 2001 HSC Specimen Paper, Aboriginal Studies, BOSTES NSW

In this example the question is worth 30 marks and the first two parts in (a) are worth 5 marks each. That leaves 20 marks for part (b), in which you would write an 'extended response'. Your essay could develop an argument based on the evidence of your Case Study.

Subject-specific tips

In many subjects in the 2019 syllabuses, the main area in which you may encounter the requirement for an extended response in essay form is in examinations set by the school itself, and in external HSC Examinations. Your key reference points for each subject, in addition to guidance from your teachers, are the relevant syllabuses, assessment and reporting guidelines, sample papers, performance-band information and other materials from the NESA website.

The assessment requirements of the new syllabuses have been devised in part to allow greater flexibility for schools in terms of what internal formal assessments can be set. Some forms that may be used are reports, multimodal presentations, digital projects, oral presentations, fieldwork presentations and literature reviews. In Society and Culture, you lodge a

Personal Interest Project, and in Science Extension you produce a Scientific Research Project. Such forms are beyond the scope of this book. However, many of the principles and microskills outlined in this book are likely to have direct application to the various forms and tasks you engage with, as they are applicable to good academic writing in general. In Ancient History, for example, 'reasoned and evidence-based arguments' are encouraged, as is a critical approach and developing one's own interpretation of evidence. Ask your teacher if you are not clear on the particular requirements of any given formal assessment.

Select glossary of instruction words

Account	Account for: state reasons for, report on Give an account of: narrate a series of events or transactions
Analyse	Identify components and the relationship between them; draw out and relate implications
Apply	Use, utilise, employ in a particular situation
Appreciate	Make a judgement about the value of
Assess	Make a judgement of value, quality, outcomes, results or size
Calculate	Ascertain/determine from given facts, figures or information
Clarify	Make clear or plain
Classify	Arrange or include in classes/categories
Compare	Show how things are similar or different
Construct	Make; build; put together items or aguments
Contrast	Show how things are different or opposite
Critically (analyse/evaluate)	Add a degree or level of accuracy, depth, knowledge and understanding, logic, questioning, reflection and quality to
Deduce	Draw conclusions
Define	State meaning and identify essential qualities

Demonstrate	Show by example
Describe	Provide characteristics and features
Discuss	Identify issues and provide points for and/or against
Distinguish	Recognise or note/indicate as being distinct or different from; to note differences between
Evaluate	Make a judgement based on criteria; determine the value of
Examine	Inquire into
Explain	Relate cause and effect; make the relationships between things evident; provide why and/or how
Extract	Choose relevant and/or appropriate details
Extrapolate	Infer from what is known
Identify	Recognise and name
Interpret	Draw meaning from
Investigate	Plan, inquire into and draw conclusions about
Justify	Support an argument or conclusion
Outline	Sketch in general terms; indicate the main features of
Predict	Suggest what may happen based on available information
Propose	Put forward (for example, a point of view, idea, argument, suggestion) for consideration or action
Recall	Present remembered ideas
Recommend	Provide reasons in favour
Recount	Retell a series of events
Summarise	Express, concisely, the relevant details
Synthesise	Put together various elements to make a whole

The above is a selection from a comprehensive glossary of instruction words available from the NESA website at www.educationstandards.nsw.edu.au.

Improve your language use

When checking over all returned work, if you don't understand why a correction was made, ask the teacher how the essay could have been improved.

- Get straight to the point! Long, vague strings of words only give the impression that you have nothing to say.
- Don't try to cram a whole paragaph into one sentence: language comes easier when you deal with thoughts one at a time.
- You can experiment by imitating writers you admire. Try to follow their style and structures, not what they are saying! Don't worry about being 'too' influenced: most writers start off emulating their heroes but the more books you read, the less debt you will owe to any one particular writer.
- Learn five spellings a day, starting with your most frequent errors.

Some practical tips

- Keep essay drafts until the assignment is finished. This can give you confidence to experiment with later drafts, knowing that you're not 'losing' previous work.

Computers

You may find it helpful to do most of your note-taking and writing on a computer.

If you have a home computer, remove all games from the hard disk (if they pose too great a temptation) and use word-processing software for your assignments. Avoid the impulse to check texts, instant messages, notifications and social media feeds frequently. Do so only at certain times of the day, when your day's work is done. Use the technology, rather than being used by it.

You may find it a good idea to save your early draft assignments under a new name, and in a subdirectory or folder named 'earlierdrafts', for example. You could save a Bruce Dawe essay as 'DAWEDRAFT1.DOC', etc. That way you can always refer back to your work rather than having to delete earlier versions and possibly deleting paragraphs that you might later decide you need. Looking at earlier drafts is often reassuring as you can measure your progress, and it is a good feeling to realise that you now have a better understanding of the topic than at the time of writing the first draft.

Make sure you back up all your files (make copies of them) and keep 'hard copies' (printouts) as well, for safety.

TIP: Some students get stuck on their original essay draft, always trying to base their next draft on the previous one, slavishly copying out whole paragraphs again under the impression that it is saving them extra work. Sometimes you are better off 'letting it go' and starting completely anew. You have nothing to lose by trying this, but by all means save the older drafts if it will help to reassure you.

Study groups

Study can be more fun, and often far more productive, if done in study groups. You can swap notes about a work or author, read each other's essays constructively, discuss language and ideas. When giving feedback to others you should:

- Emphasise the positive aspects of the essay first.
- Critically scrutinise the facts and structure, but *never* the writer.
- Never take criticism of your writing personally.

Other assistance

Some TAFEs, evening colleges and even universities offer essay-writing workshops from time to time where you can work on your skills with a group of people sharing common interests. TAFE students can enquire about assistance with learning through specialist teachers, counsellors or learning centres.

Motivation

Write a checklist outlining all the work you feel you should do in order to study each subject properly. Make a conscious decision about how much you would like to achieve. For HSC Standard English, you might plan to:

- read all texts at least twice
- write a thesis essay for each text, relating to the prescribed perspectives of the Module
- take notes on major characters and events
- gather some key quotes and relate them to your thesis
- see live productions of dramas you are studying, or their film adaptations
- find and read supplementary materials relating to the Modules where this will help
- read criticism and/or biographies of authors
- consult study guides for specific texts
- allocate the last few weeks before the exams solely to revision
- set goals for yourself to finish specific tasks by a certain (realistic) time and *stick to it*, no matter what!

And don't listen to that terrible voice of temptation whispering in your ear ... 'You can always go back and do the HSC again next year ...' Tell yourself right now 'I can't!' Who wants to lose another year of their life? Next year you could be out making money in a job, having your dream gap year or studying the course that will get you where you want to be!

Enjoyment

Although the HSC may resemble a kind of medieval torture to you, it also represents a great opportunity for you to explore the world through study, at a time when your mind is developing rapidly. Students often write much better essays on a book or poet they enjoy. Why do you think that is so?

Even if you didn't like a text at first reading, try to find something of value in it. If it's not the kind of book you would 'normally' read, open your mind and try to see what value it might have for you and for others. Talk to someone who does like that book, and find out why!

And remember, when studying an English text, that fiction, drama and poetry are written for the *enjoyment* or enlightenment of others! If you're not 'getting it' then it's worth asking yourself why not.

For teachers, marking a pile of essays can be rather hard work and it is always appreciated when a zestful, original piece comes onto the desk! Like most endeavours in life, you only get out of writing what you put into it. By now you should realise that essay writing is a skill that asks you for many inputs: your study, your writing microskills, your understanding of the essay form and your ability to express yourself clearly in language. Beyond that, your individual response will sometimes cast up a gem that your teacher will find most worthwhile and enjoyable to read. It is much more likely to happen when you are genuinely exploring the subject yourself. Good luck with your studies!

Select bibliography

The *Macquarie Dictionary* is a fine Australian dictionary. Other good dictionaries include *Chambers Twentieth Century Dictionary* and the *Oxford Concise Dictionary.*

Thesauruses

Thesauruses are helpful in looking for precise words, or an alternative word, by meaning. A classic thesaurus is Betty Kirkpatrick's *The Authorised Roget's Thesaurus*, 1998, USA, Penguin.

Grammar

Taylor, AJ 1990, *Chambers English Grammar*, Edinburgh, Chambers.

Punctuation

A short but valuable work on this important subject:

Whitaker-Wilson, C 1975, *Punctuation*, South Melbourne, Sun Books.

On Writing

Flower, L 1993, *Problem Solving Strategies for Writing*, Fort Worth, HBJ.

Klauser, H 1987, *Writing on Both Sides of the Brain*, San Francisco, Harper and Row.

Zinsser, W 1988, *Writing to Learn*, New York, Harper and Row.

NESA website

The NSW Education Standards Authority (NESA) replaced the former BOSTES NSW in January 2017. Various useful resources, including syllabuses, sample exam papers, sample student works and assessment guidelines, are available from their website: www.educationstandards.nsw.edu.au.

Notes

Notes

Notes